CHOCOLATE DESSERTS

CHOCOLATE DESSERTS

OVER 100 ESSENTIAL RECIPES
FOR THE CHOCOLATE LOVER

CIDER MILL
PRESS

BOOK
PUBLISHERS

CONTENTS

INTRODUCTION

Whether it be milk or dark, sweet, bitter, or white, the array of flavors that chocolate provides, and the number of desserts this versatility can carry, causes people all across the globe to be powerless against its sweet song.

The rare ingredient that is as comfortable playing with others as it is standing on its own, it's quite possible that chocolate is responsible for putting more smiles on people's faces than any other food, so irresistible that people routinely boast about their addictions to it.

No one is certain exactly when chocolate started to become so craveable, but it is believed that the Olmec civilization, which inhabited present-day Mexico, used cacao in a bitter, ceremonial drink, a hypothesis borne out by traces of theobromine—a stimulant that is found in chocolate and tea—being found on ancient Olmec pots and vessels.

While the exact role of chocolate in Olmec culture is impossible to pin down because they kept no written history, it appears that they passed their reverence for it onto the Mayans, who valued chocolate to the point that cocoa beans were used as currency in certain transactions.

The next great Mexican civilization, the Aztecs, carried things even further. They saw cocoa as more valuable than gold, and the mighty Aztec ruler Montezuma II supposedly drank gallons of chocolate each day, believing that it provided him with considerable energy and also served as a potent aphrodisiac.

No one is certain exactly which explorer brought this New World tradition back to Europe, with some crediting Christopher Columbus and others Hernan Cortes. Whoever is responsible, they created a sensation on the continent. Chocolate-based beverages that were sweetened with cane sugar or spruced up with spices such as cinnamon became all the rage, and fashionable houses where the wealthy congregated and indulged began popping up all over Europe by the early seventeenth century. From there, the high perch chocolate currently occupies in the culinary world was well within reach, and attained once the Swiss chocolatier Daniel Peter added dried milk powder to chocolate to create milk chocolate in 1876, and teamed with Henri Nestlé to bring milk chocolate to the masses.

Rich, creamy, sweet, bitter, slightly sour, slightly fruity, this book celebrates chocolate in all its forms, allowing chocoholics around the world to get their daily fix in a mind-boggling amount of ways. Whether it be the simple perfection of a chocolate chip cookie, the devilish decadence of chocolate cake, or a comforting cup of cocoa that you crave, this book has you covered, making it a must-have for chocolate lovers everywhere.

COOKIES & BARS

Though the ultimate chocolate-centered dessert is the subject of heated debate among the faithful, we would argue that the chocolate chip cookie will have more people fighting for its cause than any other. That level of allegiance is due in some part to the cookie's unique ability to be crisp but still moist, rich without also being heavy. When you add chocolate to the proceedings, those textures and tastes are amplified, resulting in desserts that are always simple, always magical.

Yield: 16 Cookies

Active Time: 15 Minutes

Total Time: 45 Minutes

INGREDIENTS

7 oz. unsalted butter

8¾ oz. all-purpose flour

½ teaspoon baking soda

3½ oz. sugar

5.3 oz. dark brown sugar

1 teaspoon fine sea salt

2 teaspoons pure vanilla extract

1 large egg

1 large egg yolk

1¼ cups semisweet chocolate chips

Chocolate Chip Cookies

1. Preheat the oven to 350°F. Place the butter in a saucepan and cook over medium-high heat until it is starting to brown and give off a nutty aroma (let your nose guide you here, making sure you frequently waft the steam toward you). Transfer to a heatproof mixing bowl.

2. Place the flour and baking soda in a bowl and whisk until combined.

3. Add the sugars, salt, and vanilla to the bowl containing the melted butter and whisk until combined. Add the egg and egg yolk and whisk until the mixture is smooth and thick. Add the flour-and-baking soda mixture and stir until incorporated. Add the chocolate chips and stir until evenly distributed. Form the mixture into 16 balls and place on parchment-lined baking sheets, leaving about 2 inches between each ball.

4. Working with one baking sheet at a time, place it in the oven and bake until golden brown, 12 to 16 minutes, rotating the sheet halfway through the bake time. Remove the cookies from the oven and let them cool to room temperature before serving.

Yield: 12 Cookies

Active Time: 35 Minutes

Total Time: 1 Hour and 45 Minutes

INGREDIENTS

3.2 oz. gluten-free all-purpose flour

2.6 oz. cocoa powder

½ teaspoon xanthan gum (if missing from all-purpose flour)

1 teaspoon baking soda

2 teaspoons cinnamon

½ teaspoon cayenne pepper

2 large eggs

7 oz. sugar

½ cup canola oil

1 tablespoon pure vanilla extract

1 cup chocolate chips

Gluten-Free Spicy Chocolate Cookies

1. Place the flour, cocoa powder, xanthan gum, baking soda, cinnamon, and cayenne pepper in a bowl and whisk to combine. Set the mixture aside.

2. Place the eggs, sugar, canola oil, and vanilla extract in the work bowl of a stand mixer fitted with the paddle attachment and beat on medium until the mixture is well combined.

3. Add the dry mixture to the work bowl and beat on low until the mixture comes together as a smooth dough, about 5 minutes. Add the chocolate chips and fold until combined.

4. Place the dough in the refrigerator and chill it for 1 hour.

5. Preheat the oven to 325°F. Line a baking sheet with parchment paper. Form the dough into 1½-oz. balls and place them on the baking sheet.

6. Place the cookies in the oven and bake until the edges are set, about 12 minutes. Remove the cookies from the oven, transfer them to a wire rack, and let them cool completely before enjoying.

Yield: 36 Cookies

Active Time: 20 Minutes

Total Time: 40 Minutes

INGREDIENTS

1½ cups hazelnuts, skins removed

1¼ cups bittersweet chocolate chips

3 tablespoons unsalted butter

2 tablespoons brown rice flour

2 tablespoons unsweetened cocoa powder

1 tablespoon cornstarch

¼ teaspoon gluten-free baking powder

¼ teaspoon xanthan gum

¼ teaspoon kosher salt

2 large eggs

½ cup sugar

2 tablespoons hazelnut-flavored liqueur

½ teaspoon pure vanilla extract

1 cup semisweet chocolate chips

Gluten-Free Chocolate & Hazelnut Cookies

1. Preheat the oven to 350°F and line two baking sheets with parchment paper. Place the hazelnuts on a separate baking sheet and toast for 5 to 7 minutes. Remove them from the oven and let them cool.

2. Fill a small saucepan halfway with water and bring it to a gentle simmer. Place the bittersweet chocolate chips and butter in a heatproof bowl, place it over the simmering water, and stir until the mixture is melted and smooth. Remove the mixture from heat and let it cool for 5 minutes.

3. Place the rice flour, cocoa powder, cornstarch, baking powder, xanthan gum, and salt in a mixing bowl and whisk to combine. Place the eggs, sugar, liqueur, and vanilla in a separate mixing bowl. Beat at high speed with a handheld mixer fitted with the paddle attachment until combined. Add the melted chocolate, beat to incorporate, and then gradually incorporate the dry mixture. Fold in the hazelnuts and semisweet chocolate chips.

4. Form tablespoons of the dough into balls and place them on the baking sheets. Bake for 10 to 12 minutes, until they are dry to the touch. Remove from the oven and let them cool on the baking sheets for a few minutes before transferring the cookies to wire racks to cool completely.

Gluten-Free Chocolate
& Hazelnut Cookies

see page 15

Yield: 20 Cookies

Active Time: 45 Minutes

Total Time: 2 Hours and 30 Minutes

INGREDIENTS

9 oz. dark chocolate (55 to 65 percent)

4½ oz. unsalted butter, softened

7 oz. dark brown sugar

¾ teaspoon pure vanilla extract

2 eggs

7 oz. all-purpose flour

2½ oz. cocoa powder

2 teaspoons baking powder

1 teaspoon kosher salt

2 cups confectioners' sugar, for coating

Chocolate Crinkle Cookies

1. Line two baking sheets with parchment paper. Bring water to a simmer in a small saucepan over low heat. Place the chocolate in a heatproof bowl and place the bowl over the simmering water. Occasionally stir the chocolate until it is melted. Remove the bowl from heat and set it aside.

2. In the work bowl of a stand mixer fitted with the paddle attachment, cream the butter, dark brown sugar, and vanilla on medium speed until the mixture is very light and fluffy, about 5 minutes. Scrape down the work bowl and then beat the mixture for another 5 minutes.

3. Reduce the speed to low, add the melted chocolate, and beat until incorporated, scraping down the work bowl as needed.

4. Add the eggs one at a time and beat until incorporated, again scraping the work bowl as needed. When both eggs have been incorporated, beat for another minute.

5. Add the flour, cocoa powder, baking powder, and salt and beat until the mixture comes together as a smooth dough.

6. Drop 2-oz. portions of the dough on the baking sheets, making sure to leave enough space between them. Place the baking sheets in the refrigerator and let the dough firm up for 1 hour.

7. Preheat the oven to 350°F. Place the confectioners' sugar in a mixing bowl, toss the cookie dough balls in the sugar until completely coated, and then place them back on the baking sheets.

8. Place the cookies in the oven and bake until a cake tester comes out clean after being inserted, 12 to 14 minutes.

9. Remove the cookies from the oven, transfer them to a cooling rack, and let them cool for 20 to 30 minutes before enjoying.

Yield: 48 Cookies

Active Time: 15 Minutes

Total Time: 3 Hours

INGREDIENTS

13¼ oz. all-purpose flour

1 teaspoon baking soda

1 teaspoon fine sea salt

½ lb. unsalted butter, softened

7 oz. light brown sugar

3½ oz. sugar

2 large eggs, at room temperature

2 teaspoons pure vanilla extract

1½ cups white chocolate chips

1 cup sweetened dried cranberries

White Chocolate & Cranberry Cookies

1. Place the flour, baking soda, and salt in a large mixing bowl and whisk to combine. Place the butter, brown sugar, and sugar in the work bowl of a stand mixer fitted with the paddle attachment and beat at medium speed until pale and fluffy, scraping down the sides of the bowl as needed. Reduce the speed to low and incorporate the eggs one at a time. Add the vanilla and beat to incorporate.

2. With the mixer running on low speed, gradually add the dry mixture to the wet mixture and beat until a smooth dough forms. Add the white chocolate chips and dried cranberries and fold until evenly distributed. Cover the dough with plastic wrap and refrigerate for 2 hours.

3. Preheat the oven to 350°F and line two large baking sheets with parchment paper. Drop tablespoons of the dough onto the baking sheets and, working with one baking sheet at a time, place the cookies in the oven and bake for about 10 minutes, until lightly browned. Remove from the oven and let cool on the baking sheets for 5 minutes before transferring to wire racks to cool completely.

INGREDIENTS

¾ cup sugar

1 teaspoon pure vanilla extract

7 tablespoons heavy cream

1½ oz. unsalted butter

1½ cups slivered almonds

⅓ cup candied citrus peels

⅓ cup dried cherries or plums, chopped

⅓ cup raisins

1¼ cups dark chocolate chips

Florentines

1. Place the sugar, vanilla, and cream in a saucepan and bring to a boil. Remove from heat, add the butter, and let it melt. Stir in the almonds, candied citrus peels, dried cherries or plums, and raisins.

2. Preheat the oven to 400°F and line two baking sheets with parchment paper. Place teaspoons of the mixture on the baking sheets, place the cookies in the oven, and bake for 5 to 10 minutes, until golden brown. Remove the cookies from the oven and let them cool on the baking sheets for 5 minutes before transferring to wire racks to cool completely.

3. Fill a saucepan halfway with water and bring to a gentle simmer. Place the chocolate chips in a heatproof bowl, place it over the simmering water, and stir until melted. Spread the melted chocolate on the undersides of the Florentines and let it set before serving.

INGREDIENTS

⅓ cup ground pecans

1⅔ cups confectioners' sugar

1½ cups gluten-free all-purpose flour

¾ cup gluten-free cocoa powder

½ teaspoon psyllium husks

¼ teaspoon xanthan gum

¼ teaspoon fine sea salt

½ lb. unsalted butter, chilled and cubed

1 large egg

Gluten-Free Chocolate Polvorones

1. Preheat the oven to 350°F. Line two large baking sheets with parchment paper and coat with nonstick cooking spray. In a small mixing bowl, combine the pecans and ⅔ cup of confectioners' sugar.

2. Sift the flour, cocoa powder, psyllium husks, xanthan gum, and salt in a separate mixing bowl. Add the butter and work the mixture until it comes together as a coarse, crumbly dough. Add the pecan mixture to the dough and knead to incorporate. Add the egg and knead until the dough is smooth.

3. Form the dough into small balls and place them on the baking sheets, making sure to leave enough space between them. Place the cookies in the oven and bake until the cookies are golden brown, 12 to 15 minutes.

4. Remove the cookies from the oven and let the cookies cool on the sheets for 2 minutes. Sift the remaining confectioners' sugar into a mixing bowl, roll the cookies in it until coated, and transfer to a wire rack to cool completely.

Yield: 20 Cookies

Active Time: 10 Minutes

Total Time: 1 Hour

INGREDIENTS

½ lb. unsalted butter

1½ cups almond flour

½ cup coconut flour

1½ teaspoons baking soda

2 tablespoons coconut oil, melted

½ cup stevia or preferred keto-friendly sweetener

2 teaspoons pure vanilla extract

½ lb. sugar-free semisweet chocolate chips

Keto Chocolate Chip Cookies

1. Preheat the oven to 350°F and line two baking sheets with parchment paper. Place the butter in a saucepan and cook over medium-high heat until it is dark brown and has a nutty aroma. Transfer the browned butter to a heatproof mixing bowl and set it aside.

2. Place the flours and baking soda in a mixing bowl and whisk until combined. Set the mixture aside.

3. Add the coconut oil, sweetener, and vanilla to the bowl containing the melted butter and whisk until combined. Gradually add the dry mixture and stir until the mixture comes together as a dough. Add the chocolate chips and fold until evenly distributed. Form tablespoons of the mixture into balls and place them on the parchment-lined baking sheets, leaving about 2 inches between each ball. Gently press down on the balls to flatten them slightly.

4. Place the cookies in the oven and bake, rotating the sheets halfway through, until they are golden brown, about 12 minutes. Remove the cookies from the oven and let them cool on the baking sheets for 10 minutes before transferring to wire racks to cool completely.

Nutritional Info Per Serving: Calories: 178; Fat: 16.5 g; Net Carbs: 5.1 g; Protein: 2.5 g

Keto Chocolate Chip Cookies
see page 25

Yield: 18 Cookies

Active Time: 15 Minutes

Total Time: 1 Hour

INGREDIENTS

1¼ cups almond flour

½ cup gluten-free cocoa powder

1 teaspoon gluten-free baking soda

¼ teaspoon fine sea salt

1 cup dark chocolate chunks

1 large egg, at room temperature

¼ cup sugar

½ cup brown sugar

4 oz. unsalted butter, softened

1 teaspoon pure vanilla extract

Gluten-Free Double Chocolate Cookies

1. Preheat the oven to 350°F. Line two baking sheets with parchment paper and coat with nonstick cooking spray. In a mixing bowl, combine the almond flour, cocoa powder, baking soda, and salt.

2. Fill a small saucepan halfway with water and bring it to a simmer. Place half of the chocolate in a heatproof bowl, place it over the simmering water, and stir until melted and smooth.

3. In the work bowl of a stand mixer fitted with the paddle attachment, cream the egg, sugars, butter, and vanilla on medium speed until the mixture is very light and fluffy, about 5 minutes. Add the melted chocolate and gently stir to incorporate. Add the almond flour mixture and remaining chocolate and beat until the mixture comes together as a soft cookie dough.

4. Drop teaspoons of the dough on the baking sheets, making sure to leave enough space between them. Place in the oven and bake until set, 10 to 12 minutes. Remove from the oven and let the cookies cool on the sheets for a few minutes before transferring to a wire rack to cool completely.

Yield: 24 Cookies

Active Time: 30 Minutes

Total Time: 3 Hours and 30 Minutes

INGREDIENTS

13.2 oz. all-purpose flour, plus more as needed

⅔ cup sugar

½ teaspoon fine sea salt

¾ teaspoon baking powder

½ teaspoon baking soda

1 teaspoon cinnamon

6 oz. unsalted butter, divided into tablespoons

3 large eggs, lightly beaten

12 large marshmallows, halved

2 cups dark chocolate chips

1 tablespoon coconut oil

Chocolate-Covered Marshmallow Cookies

1. Place the flour, sugar, salt, baking powder, baking soda, and cinnamon in a mixing bowl and whisk to combine. Add the butter and work the mixture with a pastry blender until it is coarse crumbs. Add the eggs and stir until a stiff dough forms. Shape the dough into a ball, cover with plastic wrap, and refrigerate for 1 hour.

2. Preheat the oven to 375°F and line two baking sheets with parchment paper. Place the dough on a flour-dusted work surface and roll out to ¼ inch thick. Cut the dough into 24 rounds and place them on the baking sheets.

3. Place in the oven and bake for about 10 minutes, until the edges have browned. Remove from the oven and transfer the cookies to wire racks to cool completely. Leave the oven on.

4. When the cookies are cool, place a marshmallow half on each cookie. Place them back in the oven and, while keeping a close eye on the cookies, bake until the marshmallows start to slump. Remove the cookies from the oven and let them cool completely on the baking sheets.

5. Bring water to a simmer in a small saucepan over low heat. Place the chocolate in a heatproof bowl and place the bowl over the simmering water. Occasionally stir the chocolate until it is melted. Remove the bowl from heat, add the coconut oil to the melted chocolate, and stir until incorporated.

6. Drop the cookies into the chocolate, turning to coat all sides. Carefully remove the coated cookies with a fork, hold them over the bowl to let any excess chocolate drip off, and place them on pieces of parchment paper. Let the chocolate set before serving.

Yield: 12 Cookies

Active Time: 40 Minutes

Total Time: 2 Hours

INGREDIENTS

6.7 oz. all-purpose flour, plus more as needed

1½ oz. unsweetened cocoa powder

½ teaspoon instant espresso powder

¼ teaspoon fine sea salt

½ lb. unsalted butter, divided into tablespoons and softened

3 oz. confectioners' sugar, sifted

2½ oz. fine almond flour

1 teaspoon pure vanilla extract

½ cup white chocolate chips

Kipferl Biscuits

1. Place all of the ingredients, except for the white chocolate chips, in the work bowl of a stand mixer fitted with the paddle attachment and beat at medium speed until the mixture comes together as a soft dough. Flatten the dough into a disc, cover it with plastic wrap, and refrigerate for 1 hour.

2. Preheat the oven to 350°F and line two large baking sheets with parchment paper. Remove the dough from the refrigerator and let it stand at room temperature for 5 minutes. Place the dough on a flour-dusted work surface, roll it into a ¾-inch-thick log, cut it into 2-inch-long pieces, and roll them into cylinders with your hands, while tapering and curling the ends to create crescent shapes. Place them on the baking sheets.

3. Place the biscuits in the oven and bake until they are set and firm, about 15 minutes. Remove the biscuits from the oven and transfer them to wire racks to cool.

4. Fill a small saucepan halfway with water and bring it to a gentle simmer. Place the white chocolate chips in a heatproof bowl, place it over the simmering water, and stir until melted. Drizzle the melted white chocolate over the cooled biscuits and let it set before serving.

INGREDIENTS

2 tablespoons ground flaxseed

⅓ cup real maple syrup

1 teaspoon pure vanilla extract

1 (14 oz.) can of black beans, drained and rinsed

2 tablespoons coconut oil

⅓ cup cocoa powder

¼ teaspoon fine sea salt

¼ teaspoon cayenne pepper

½ cup chopped dark chocolate (70 percent)

Zest of 1 lime

Vegan Cayenne, Lime & Chocolate Cookies

1. Preheat the oven to 375°F. Line a large baking sheet with parchment paper. Combine the flaxseed, maple syrup, and vanilla in a mixing bowl. Place the black beans, coconut oil, cocoa powder, salt, and cayenne in a food processor and blitz until well combined. Add the maple syrup mixture and pulse until the mixture is a wet dough that can hold its shape.

2. Transfer the dough to a mixing bowl and stir in the chocolate and lime zest. Drop tablespoons of the dough onto the baking sheet, making sure to leave enough space between them.

3. Press down on the cookies to flatten them slightly, place them in the oven, and bake until they are just firm, 10 to 15 minutes. Remove the cookies from the oven and let them cool on the baking sheet for a few minutes before transferring them to a cooling rack to cool completely.

INGREDIENTS

1 (14 oz.) can of sweetened condensed milk

7 oz. sweetened shredded coconut

7 oz. unsweetened shredded coconut

¼ teaspoon kosher salt

½ teaspoon pure vanilla extract

2 egg whites

Chocolate Ganache (see page 258), warm

Coconut Macaroons

1. Line a baking sheet with parchment paper. In a mixing bowl, mix the sweetened condensed milk, shredded coconut, salt, and vanilla together with a rubber spatula until combined. Set the mixture aside.

2. In the work bowl of a stand mixer fitted with the whisk attachment, whip the egg whites until they hold stiff peaks. Add the whipped egg whites to the coconut mixture and fold to incorporate.

3. Scoop 2-oz. portions of the mixture onto the baking sheet, making sure to leave enough space between them. Place the baking sheet in the refrigerator and let the dough firm up for 1 hour.

4. Preheat the oven to 350°F.

5. Place the cookies in the oven and bake until they are lightly golden brown, 20 to 25 minutes.

6. Remove the cookies from the oven, transfer them to a cooling rack, and let them cool for 1 hour.

7. Dip the bottoms of the macaroons into the ganache and then place them back on the baking sheet. If desired, drizzle some of the ganache over the tops of the cookies. Refrigerate until the chocolate is set, about 5 minutes, before serving.

Coconut Macaroons

see page 35

Yield: 36 Cookies

Active Time: 20 Minutes

Total Time: 45 Minutes

INGREDIENTS

2 tablespoons instant coffee grounds

2 tablespoons boiling water

½ cup vegetable shortening

2 cups confectioners' sugar

¼ cup silken tofu

½ teaspoon pure vanilla extract

¼ cup unsweetened cocoa powder

⅔ cup all-purpose flour

⅔ cup whole wheat pastry flour

Pinch of kosher salt

Vegan Crinkle Cookies

1. Preheat the oven to 350°F and line two baking sheets with parchment paper. Place the instant coffee and boiling water in a small bowl and stir to dissolve the coffee. Let the mixture cool.

2. Place the shortening and ½ cup of the confectioners' sugar in the work bowl of a stand mixer fitted with the paddle attachment and beat until the mixture is light and fluffy. Add the tofu and vanilla and beat until incorporated. Add the cocoa powder and instant coffee and beat until thoroughly incorporated. With the mixer running at low speed, gradually add the flours and salt and beat until the dough just holds together.

3. Form tablespoons of the dough into balls and place them on the baking sheets. Place them in the oven and bake until they are firm and starting to crack, 15 to 18 minutes.

4. Remove the cookies from the oven and let them cool on the baking sheets for 2 minutes. Sift the remaining confectioners' sugar into a shallow dish and roll the cookies in the sugar until coated.

5. Transfer the cookies to wire racks to cool completely.

Yield: 12 Cookies

Active Time: 15 Minutes

Total Time: 1 Hour

INGREDIENTS

½ cup vegan butter

½ cup sugar

½ cup brown sugar

1 teaspoon pure vanilla extract

1 cup all-purpose flour, plus more as needed

⅔ cup cocoa powder

1 teaspoon baking soda

¼ teaspoon fine sea salt

1 tablespoon soy milk

½ cup vegan chocolate chips

Vegan Double Chocolate Cookies

1. Preheat the oven to 350°F. Line two baking sheets with parchment paper. In the work bowl of a stand mixer fitted with the paddle attachment, cream the butter, sugar, brown sugar, and vanilla on medium speed until the mixture is very light and fluffy, about 5 minutes.

2. Sift the flour, cocoa powder, baking soda, and salt into a separate mixing bowl. Gradually add the flour mixture to the creamed butter and beat until incorporated. Add the soy milk and beat until the mixture comes together as a thick dough. Add the vegan chocolate chips and beat until evenly distributed.

3. Form the mixture into 12 balls and arrange them on the baking sheets, making sure to leave enough space between.

4. Flatten the cookies slightly, place them in the oven, and bake until they are set and cracked on top, about 15 minutes.

5. Remove the cookies from the oven, place the baking sheets on wire racks, and let the cookies cool on the sheets.

INGREDIENTS

¾ cup whole milk

7 oz. sugar

¼ teaspoon fine sea salt

4 oz. dark chocolate, chopped

1 teaspoon pure vanilla extract

½ cup creamy peanut butter

1 cup rolled oats

Chewy Peanut Butter & Oat Bars

1. Place the milk, sugar, and salt in a small saucepan and whisk to combine. Cook over medium heat until the mixture comes to a boil and thickens, approximately 10 minutes. Remove the pan from heat.

2. Fill a small saucepan halfway with water and bring to a gentle simmer. Place the chocolate in a heatproof bowl, place it over the simmering water, and stir until it has melted. Remove the bowl from heat.

3. Add the vanilla, one-quarter of the melted chocolate, and the peanut butter to the pan and stir until well combined. Fold in the oats and stir until they are completely coated.

4. Line a square 8-inch cake pan with parchment paper and pour the contents of the saucepan into it. Press the mixture into an even layer, spread the remaining melted chocolate over the top, and let the mixture sit for 30 minutes.

5. Cut the mixture into little bars and serve immediately, or store in the refrigerator until ready to serve.

Yield: 24 Cookies

Active Time: 15 Minutes

Total Time: 1 Hour

INGREDIENTS

2⅓ cups spelt flour

1 tablespoon flaxseed meal

1 teaspoon baking soda

1 teaspoon cinnamon

½ teaspoon ground ginger

½ teaspoon fine sea salt

¼ teaspoon freshly grated nutmeg

¼ teaspoon cardamom

1 cup pumpkin puree

½ cup vegan butter, melted

¼ cup real maple syrup

⅓ cup coconut sugar

1 tablespoon unsalted creamy almond butter

1 cup vegan chocolate chips

Vegan Pumpkin & Chocolate Chip Cookies

1. Preheat the oven to 350°F. Line two baking sheets with parchment paper. In a large bowl, combine the flour, flaxseed meal, baking soda, cinnamon, ginger, salt, nutmeg, and cardamom.

2. In the work bowl of a stand mixer fitted with the paddle attachment, combine the pumpkin puree, vegan butter, maple syrup, coconut sugar, and almond butter and beat until smooth. Add the wet mixture to the dry mixture and stir until the mixture just comes together as a dough. Add the chocolate chips and fold to incorporate.

3. Drop 2-tablespoon portions of the dough on the baking sheets, making sure to leave enough space between them. Flatten the cookies, place them in the oven, and bake until they are firm with lightly browned edges, about 10 minutes.

4. Remove the cookies from the oven and let them rest on the baking sheets for a few minutes before transferring them to a cooling rack to cool completely.

Yield: 20 Cookies

Active Time: 30 Minutes

Total Time: 2 Hours and 15 Minutes

INGREDIENTS

½ lb. unsalted butter, softened

1 lb. sugar

2 eggs

¾ teaspoon pure vanilla extract

9½ oz. all-purpose flour

4½ oz. cocoa powder

1½ teaspoons baking soda

½ teaspoon baking powder

¾ teaspoon kosher salt

1 cup **Butterfluff Filling** (see page 255)

Chocolate Sandwich Cookies

1. Line two baking sheets with parchment paper. In the work bowl of a stand mixer fitted with the paddle attachment, cream the butter and sugar on medium until the mixture is light and fluffy, about 5 minutes. Scrape down the work bowl with a rubber spatula and beat the mixture for another 5 minutes.

2. Reduce the speed to low, add the eggs one at a time, and beat until incorporated, again scraping the work bowl as needed. When both eggs have been incorporated, scrape down the work bowl, add the vanilla, and beat for another minute.

3. Add the flour, cocoa powder, baking soda, baking powder, and salt and beat on low until the dough comes together.

4. Drop 1-oz. portions of the dough on the baking sheets, making sure to leave enough space between them. Place the baking sheets in the refrigerator and let the dough firm up for 1 hour.

5. Preheat the oven to 350°F.

6. Place the cookies in the oven and bake until they are starting to firm up, about 8 minutes.

7. Remove the cookies from the oven, transfer them to a cooling rack, and let them cool for 20 to 30 minutes.

8. Place the filling in a piping bag and cut a ½-inch hole in the bag. Pipe about 1 tablespoon of filling on half of the cookies. Use the other halves to assemble the sandwich and enjoy.

Yield: 12 Bars

Active Time: 15 Minutes

Total Time: 1 Hour and 15 Minutes

INGREDIENTS

¾ lb. marshmallow creme

4½ oz. unsalted butter

2 tablespoons matcha powder

¾ teaspoon fine sea salt

9 cups crispy rice cereal

¾ teaspoon pure vanilla extract

2½ cups white chocolate chips

White Chocolate & Matcha Rice Krispies Treats

1. Line a 13 x 9–inch baking pan with parchment paper and coat it with nonstick cooking spray.

2. Fill a small saucepan halfway with water and bring it to a simmer. Place the marshmallow creme, butter, matcha powder, and salt in a heatproof mixing bowl, place it over the simmering water, and stir the mixture with a rubber spatula until the butter has melted and the mixture is thoroughly combined. Remove the bowl from heat, add the cereal, and fold until combined. Add the vanilla and white chocolate chips and fold until evenly distributed.

3. Transfer the mixture to the baking pan and spread it with a rubber spatula. Place another piece of parchment over the mixture and pack it down with your hand until it is flat and even. Remove the top piece of parchment.

4. Place the pan in the refrigerator for 1 hour.

5. Run a knife along the edge of the pan and turn the mixture out onto a cutting board. Cut it into squares and enjoy.

Yield: 24 Cookies

Active Time: 30 Minutes

Total Time: 2 Hours

INGREDIENTS

4 oz. unsalted butter, softened

4 oz. smooth peanut butter

½ lb. sugar

½ lb. dark brown sugar

1½ teaspoons kosher salt

1 teaspoon baking soda

2 eggs

1½ teaspoons pure vanilla extract

14½ oz. all-purpose flour

14 oz. semisweet chocolate chips

Peanut Butter & Chocolate Chip Cookies

1. Line two baking sheets with parchment paper. In the work bowl of a stand mixer fitted with the paddle attachment, cream the butter, peanut butter, sugar, dark brown sugar, salt, and baking soda on medium speed until the mixture is very light and fluffy, about 5 minutes. Scrape down the work bowl and then beat the mixture for another 5 minutes.

2. Add the eggs one at a time and beat until incorporated, again scraping the work bowl as needed. When both eggs have been incorporated, scrape down the work bowl, add the vanilla, and beat for another minute. Add the flour and chocolate chips and beat until the mixture comes together as a dough.

3. Drop 2-oz. portions of the dough on the baking sheets, making sure to leave enough space between them. Place the baking sheets in the refrigerator and let the dough firm up for 1 hour.

4. Preheat the oven to 350°F.

5. Place the cookies in the oven and bake until they are lightly golden brown around their edges, 10 to 12 minutes. Do not let the cookies become fully brown or they will end up being too crispy.

6. Remove the cookies from the oven, transfer them to a cooling rack, and let them cool for 20 to 30 minutes before enjoying.

Peanut Butter & Chocolate Chip Cookies
see page 49

Yield: 24 Cookies

Active Time: 20 Minutes

Total Time: 2 Hours

INGREDIENTS

½ lb. unsalted butter, softened

½ lb. sugar

½ lb. dark brown sugar

1½ teaspoons kosher salt

1 teaspoon baking soda

2 eggs

1½ teaspoons pure vanilla extract

14½ oz. all-purpose flour

7 oz. macadamia nuts, toasted

7 oz. white chocolate chips

White Chocolate Chip & Macadamia Cookies

1. Line two baking sheets with parchment paper. In the work bowl of a stand mixer fitted with the paddle attachment, cream the butter, sugar, dark brown sugar, salt, and baking soda on medium speed until the mixture is very light and fluffy, about 5 minutes. Scrape down the work bowl and then beat the mixture for another 5 minutes.

2. Reduce the speed to low, add the eggs one at a time, and beat until incorporated, again scraping the work bowl as needed. When both eggs have been incorporated, scrape down the work bowl, add the vanilla, raise the speed to medium, and beat for 1 minute.

3. Add the flour, macadamia nuts, and white chocolate chips, reduce the speed to low, and beat until the dough comes together.

4. Drop 2-oz. portions of the dough on the baking sheets, making sure to leave enough space between them. Place the baking sheets in the refrigerator and let the dough firm up for 1 hour.

5. Preheat the oven to 350°F.

6. Place the cookies in the oven and bake until they are lightly golden brown around their edges, 10 to 12 minutes. Remove the cookies from the oven, transfer them to a cooling rack, and let them cool for 20 to 30 minutes before enjoying.

Yield: 24 Cookies

Active Time: 45 Minutes

Total Time: 3 Hours

INGREDIENTS

2½ oz. all-purpose flour

2 tablespoons cocoa powder

5 egg whites

4½ oz. confectioners' sugar

½ teaspoon pure vanilla extract

5.3 oz. unsalted butter

Chocolate Tuiles

1. Sift the flour and cocoa powder into a small bowl and set the mixture aside.

2. In a medium bowl, whisk the egg whites, confectioners' sugar, and vanilla together. Set the mixture aside.

3. In a small saucepan, melt the butter over low heat. Stir it into the egg white mixture, add the flour mixture, and whisk until the mixture is a smooth batter. Cover the bowl with plastic wrap and place in the refrigerator for 2 hours.

4. Preheat the oven to 400°F.

5. Line an 18 x 13–inch baking sheet with a Silpat mat. Place 2-teaspoon portions of the batter about 5 inches apart from one another. Use a small, offset spatula to spread the batter into 4-inch circles. Tap the pan lightly on the counter to remove any air bubbles and level the circles.

6. Place the tuiles in the oven and bake until their edges begin to curl up, 4 to 5 minutes. Remove the tuiles from the oven. Working quickly, carefully remove them with the offset spatula and transfer them immediately to a cooling rack.

7. Repeat until all of the batter has been used.

Yield: 18 Cookies

Active Time: 30 Minutes

Total Time: 2 Hours

INGREDIENTS

7.7 oz. dark chocolate (55 to 65 percent)

1.1 oz. unsalted butter, softened

2 eggs

3.6 oz. sugar

¾ teaspoon pure vanilla extract

1¼ oz. all-purpose flour

¼ teaspoon baking powder

¼ teaspoon kosher salt

¼ cup espresso powder

6 oz. chocolate chips

Double Shot Cookies

1. Line two baking sheets with parchment paper. Fill a small saucepan halfway with water and bring it to a simmer. Place the dark chocolate and butter in a heatproof bowl, place it over the simmering water, and stir until they have melted and been combined. Remove from heat and whisk in the eggs, sugar, and vanilla.

2. Add the flour, baking powder, salt, and espresso powder and whisk until the dough comes together. Add the chocolate chips and fold until evenly distributed.

3. Drop 2-oz. portions of the dough on the baking sheets, making sure to leave enough space between them. Place the baking sheets in the refrigerator and let the dough firm up for 1 hour.

4. Preheat the oven to 350°F.

5. Place the cookies in the oven and bake until a cake tester inserted into their centers comes out clean, 12 to 14 minutes.

6. Remove the cookies from the oven, transfer them to a cooling rack, and let them cool for 20 to 30 minutes before enjoying.

Yield: 20 Cookies

Active Time: 30 Minutes

Total Time: 2 Hours

INGREDIENTS

9 oz. Mexican chocolate

4½ oz. unsalted butter, softened

7 oz. dark brown sugar

¾ teaspoon pure vanilla extract

2 eggs

7 oz. all-purpose flour

2½ oz. cocoa powder

2 teaspoons baking powder

½ teaspoon cinnamon

¼ teaspoon ancho chile powder

1 teaspoon kosher salt

2 cups confectioners' sugar, for coating

Mexican Chocolate Crinkle Cookies

1. Line two baking sheets with parchment paper. Fill a small saucepan halfway with water and bring it to a simmer. Place the chocolate in a heatproof bowl, place it over the simmering water, and stir until melted. Remove from heat and set aside.

2. In the work bowl of a stand mixer fitted with the paddle attachment, cream the butter, brown sugar, and vanilla on medium speed until the mixture is very light and fluffy, about 5 minutes. Scrape down the work bowl and then beat the mixture for another 5 minutes.

3. Reduce the speed to low, add the melted chocolate, and beat until incorporated.

4. Incorporate the eggs one at a time, again scraping the work bowl as needed. When both eggs have been incorporated, scrape down the work bowl. Set the speed to medium and beat for 1 minute.

5. Add the flour, cocoa powder, baking powder, cinnamon, ancho chile powder, and salt, reduce the speed to low, and beat until the mixture comes together as a dough.

6. Drop 2-oz. portions of the dough on the baking sheets, making sure to leave enough space between them. Place the baking sheets in the refrigerator and let the dough firm up for 1 hour.

7. Preheat the oven to 350°F. Place the confectioners' sugar in a mixing bowl, toss the cookie dough balls in the sugar until completely coated, and then place them back on the baking sheets.

8. Place the cookies in the oven and bake until a cake tester inserted into their centers comes out clean, 12 to 14 minutes.

9. Remove the cookies from the oven, transfer them to a cooling rack, and let them cool for 20 to 30 minutes before enjoying.

Yield: 12 Bars

Active Time: 30 Minutes

Total Time: 2 Hours and 30 Minutes

INGREDIENTS

6 cups crispy rice cereal

3 cups rolled oats

4 cups chocolate chips

1 cup dark brown sugar

6 oz. unsalted butter

¾ cup honey

¼ cup light corn syrup

4 teaspoons kosher salt

2 tablespoons pure vanilla extract

2 cups Chocolate Ganache (see page 258), warm

Crispy Rice, Oat & Chocolate Bars

1. Line a 13 x 9–inch baking pan with parchment paper and coat it with nonstick cooking spray. Place the cereal, oats, and 2 cups of the chocolate chips in a mixing bowl and stir to combine. Set the mixture aside.

2. In a medium saucepan, combine the brown sugar, butter, honey, corn syrup, and salt. Bring to a boil over medium heat and cook for another 2 minutes. Remove the pan from heat, whisk in the vanilla, and then pour it over the cereal mixture. Stir with a rubber spatula until combined.

3. Transfer the mixture to the baking pan and press down on it until it is flat and even. Sprinkle the remaining chocolate chips over the mixture and gently press them down into it. Place the baking pan in the refrigerator for 2 hours.

4. Remove the pan from the refrigerator and cut the mixture into bars.

5. Drizzle the ganache over the bars and enjoy.

Yield: 15 Cookies

Active Time: 40 Minutes

Total Time: 1 Hour

INGREDIENTS

17.6 oz. all-purpose flour, plus more as needed

5.3 oz. almond flour

5.3 oz. honey

5.3 oz. sugar

1½ teaspoons baker's ammonia

2 teaspoons Pisto (see page 261)

1.2 oz. unsweetened cocoa powder

Zest and juice of 1 orange

3½ oz. hot water (140°F), plus more as needed

7 oz. bittersweet chocolate, chopped

Mostaccioli

1. Preheat the oven to 350°F and line two baking sheets with parchment paper. Place the flours, honey, sugar, baker's ammonia, Pisto, cocoa powder, orange zest, and orange juice in the work bowl of a stand mixer fitted with the paddle attachment. With the mixer running, gradually add the hot water and work the mixture until it comes together as a soft, smooth dough. Depending on the all-purpose flour you end up using, you may not need to use all of the water; you also may need to add more water if the dough is too stiff.

2. Place the dough on a flour-dusted work surface and roll it out until it is about ½ inch thick. Cut the dough into rectangles and place them on the baking sheets.

3. Place the cookies in the oven and bake until they are golden brown, 10 to 15 minutes. Remove the cookies from the oven and let them cool.

4. While the cookies are cooling, bring a few inches of water to a simmer in a medium saucepan. Place the chocolate in a heatproof bowl, place it over the simmering water, and stir until the chocolate has melted.

5. Using kitchen tongs, dip the cookies into the melted chocolate and place them on wire racks. Let the chocolate set before serving.

WHITE CHOCOLATE

While some apocryphal tales assert that white chocolate is the result of cocoa beans that have not been roasted, that is far from the case. White chocolate is instead made with cocoa butter (a product resulting from roasted cocoa beans), sugar, and milk powder. As it does not contain the cocoa mass that is produced by grinding the roasted nibs of the cacao bean finely, some do not consider white chocolate to be a true chocolate.

Yield: 16 Bars

Active Time: 10 Minutes

Total Time: 1 Hour

INGREDIENTS

1 cup blanched and chopped almonds

1 cup unsalted butter

1 cup packed dark brown sugar

1 large egg yolk, at room temperature

1 teaspoon pure vanilla extract

2 cups all-purpose flour

¼ teaspoon fine sea salt

½ lb. quality white chocolate, chopped

White Chocolate Almond Bars

1. Preheat the oven to 350°F and line a 13 x 9–inch baking dish with parchment paper. Place the almonds on a baking sheet, place them in the oven, and toast until they are lightly browned, 5 to 7 minutes.

2. Place the butter and brown sugar in the work bowl of a stand mixer fitted with the paddle attachment and cream at medium speed until the mixture is light and fluffy.

3. Add the egg yolk and vanilla and beat for 1 minute. Gradually add the flour and salt and beat until the mixture comes together as a stiff dough.

4. Place the dough in the baking dish, gently pat it into an even layer, and prick it with a fork. Place the pan in the oven and bake until the crust is light brown, about 20 minutes.

5. Remove the pan from the oven and scatter the white chocolate evenly over the crust. Return the pan to the oven for 1 minute, remove, and spread the white chocolate into an even layer. Sprinkle the toasted almonds on top and let the mixture cool.

6. Cut the mixture into bars and enjoy.

Yield: 12 Bars

Active Time: 1 Hour

Total Time: 3 Hours and 30 Minutes

INGREDIENTS

For the Crust

½ lb. dark chocolate (55 to 65 percent)

4 oz. unsalted butter

6 oz. sugar

2 oz. light brown sugar

2 tablespoons cocoa powder

¼ teaspoon kosher salt

3 eggs

¾ teaspoon pure vanilla extract

For the Topping

28½ oz. confectioners' sugar

6 tablespoons unsalted butter, softened

½ cup heavy cream

2 cups peppermint candy pieces, plus more for topping

2 cups Chocolate Ganache (see page 258), warm

Peppermint Bars

1. Preheat the oven to 350°F. Line a 13 x 9–inch baking pan with parchment paper and coat it with nonstick cooking spray. To begin preparations for the crust, fill a small saucepan halfway with water and bring it to a simmer. Place the chocolate and butter in a heatproof bowl, place it over the simmering water, and stir until they are melted and combined. Remove from heat and set aside.

2. In a mixing bowl, whisk the sugar, brown sugar, cocoa powder, and salt together, making sure to break up any clumps. Add the eggs and vanilla, whisk to incorporate, and then add the melted chocolate mixture. Whisk to incorporate, pour the batter into the baking pan, and even the surface with a rubber spatula. Lightly tap the baking pan on the counter to settle the batter and remove any air bubbles.

3. Place in the oven and bake until a cake tester comes out clean, 20 to 30 minutes. Remove from the oven and transfer the pan to a cooling rack.

4. To prepare the topping, place the confectioners' sugar, butter, and heavy cream in the work bowl of a stand mixer fitted with the paddle attachment and cream on low until the mixture comes together. Raise the speed to medium and beat until light and fluffy. Add the peppermint candies and beat until just incorporated.

5. Spread the mixture over the baked crust, using an offset spatula to even it out. Transfer the pan to the refrigerator and chill until the topping is set, about 2 hours.

6. Run a sharp knife along the edge of the pan and carefully remove the bars. Place them on a cutting board and cut. Drizzle the ganache over the bars, sprinkle the additional peppermint candies on top, and store in the refrigerator until ready to serve.

INGREDIENTS

For the Cookies

1 cup unsalted butter

¼ cup sugar

1 large egg yolk, at room temperature

½ teaspoon pure vanilla extract

½ teaspoon baking powder

½ teaspoon fine sea salt

½ cup cocoa powder

2 cups all-purpose flour

½ cup semisweet chocolate chips, melted

For the Filling

½ cup heavy cream

1½ tablespoons light corn syrup

¾ lb. quality white chocolate, minced

2 tablespoons unsalted butter

1 teaspoon mint extract

¼ teaspoon red or green food coloring (optional)

Grasshopper Cookies

1. To begin preparations for the cookies, place the butter and sugar in the work bowl of a stand mixer fitted with the paddle attachment and cream the mixture until it is light and fluffy.

2. Add the egg yolk, vanilla, baking powder, and salt and beat to incorporate them. Gradually add the cocoa powder and flour and beat until the mixture comes together as a stiff dough.

3. Place the dough on a sheet of parchment paper and roll it into a 2½-inch-thick log. Cover the dough with plastic wrap and chill it in the refrigerator for 2 hours.

4. To prepare the filling, place the cream and corn syrup in a small saucepan and bring to a simmer. Stir in the white chocolate, butter, and mint extract, cover the pan, and remove it from heat. Let the mixture sit for 5 minutes. Stir until smooth and, if using, stir in the food coloring. Press plastic wrap directly onto the surface of the filling and chill it in the refrigerator.

5. Preheat the oven to 350°F. Line two baking sheets with parchment paper and cut the chilled dough into ½-inch-thick slices. Place the cookies on the baking sheets, place them in the oven, and bake until the edges start to brown, about 10 minutes. Remove the cookies from the oven, let them cool on the baking sheets for 10 minutes, and then transfer them to a wire rack to cool completely.

6. When the cookies are cool, beat the filling with a handheld mixer until it is light and fluffy. Place a dollop on the flat side of a cookie and top with another cookie. Repeat until all of the cookies and filling have been used.

7. Dip the cookies in the melted chocolate until completely coated. Place the cookies back on the baking sheets and chill them in the refrigerator until the chocolate has set, about 20 minutes.

Grasshopper Cookies
see page 67

Yield: 16 Bars

Active Time: 15 Minutes

Total Time: 1 Hour

INGREDIENTS

1 cup unsalted butter, plus more as needed

¾ cup sugar

¾ cup packed light brown sugar

2 large eggs, at room temperature

1 teaspoon pure almond extract

¼ cup cocoa powder

1 teaspoon baking soda

½ teaspoon fine sea salt

2 cups all-purpose flour

1 cup miniature chocolate chips

1 (14 oz.) can of sweetened condensed milk

1 cup unsweetened shredded coconut

Chocolate & Coconut Bars

1. Preheat the oven to 375°F and coat a 13 x 9–inch baking dish with butter. Combine the butter, sugar, and brown sugar in the work bowl of a stand mixer fitted with the paddle attachment and cream the mixture until it is light and fluffy.

2. Add the eggs and almond extract and beat until well combined. Add the cocoa powder, baking soda, and salt and beat at medium speed. Reduce the speed to low, add the flour, beat until the mixture comes together as a smooth batter, and then fold in the chocolate chips.

3. Spread the batter in the baking dish in an even layer. Place the condensed milk and coconut in a small bowl and stir to combine. Spread this mixture in an even layer on top of the batter.

4. Place the dish in the oven and bake until a cake tester inserted into the center comes out clean, 25 to 30 minutes.

5. Remove the baking dish from the oven and let the mixture cool before cutting it into bars.

CAKES, BROWNIES & BREADS

When you are in need of something that can comfort, or something worthy of serving as the centerpiece of a celebration, the recipes in this chapter are where you should turn. Whether you want the grand decadence that only a chocolate cake can supply, the irresistible nostalgia of a cream-filled cupcake, the incredible balance of richness and lightness that only a brioche possesses, or some other classic chocolate-based confection, you're sure to find it here.

Yield: 16 Brownies

Active Time: 25 Minutes

Total Time: 1 Hour and 15 Minutes

INGREDIENTS

¾ cup unsalted butter, softened, plus more as needed

3 oz. bittersweet chocolate, chopped

¼ cup heavy cream, plus more as needed

1 cup all-purpose flour

3 tablespoons cocoa powder

½ teaspoon fine sea salt

2½ cups confectioners' sugar

2 large eggs

½ teaspoon pure vanilla extract

2 to 4 drops of red food coloring (optional)

¾ cup crushed peppermint candies

Peppermint Brownies

1. Preheat the oven to 350°F and coat a square 8-inch baking dish with butter. Fill a small saucepan halfway with water and bring it to a simmer. Place the chocolate and cream in a heatproof bowl, place it over the simmering water, and stir until the chocolate has melted and the mixture is smooth. Remove the pan from heat and set it aside.

2. Place the flour, cocoa powder, and salt in a mixing bowl and whisk until combined. Place two-thirds of the butter and ½ cup of the sugar in the work bowl of a stand mixer fitted with the paddle attachment and beat until the mixture is light and fluffy. Incorporate the eggs one at a time and then add the chocolate-and-cream mixture and vanilla.

3. Gradually add the flour-and-cocoa mixture and beat until the mixture comes together as a smooth batter.

4. Place the batter in the baking dish, place it in the oven, and bake until the brownies are firm and a toothpick inserted into the center comes out clean, 30 to 40 minutes.

5. Remove the brownies from the oven and let them cool in the pan.

6. While the brownies are cooling, place the remaining butter, sugar, and cream in the work bowl of the stand mixer and beat until the mixture is light and fluffy. If using, add the red food coloring and beat until incorporated. Add cream in 1-teaspoon increments if the frosting is too thick.

7. Spread the frosting over the cooled brownies, sprinkle the crushed peppermint candies on top, cut them into small bars, and enjoy.

Yield: 8 Servings

Active Time: 10 Minutes

Total Time: 1 Hour and 30 Minutes

INGREDIENTS

½ cup unsalted butter, melted, plus more as needed

6 eggs

1⅓ cups sugar

½ cup sour cream

1 teaspoon orange zest

1⅓ cups cake flour

⅔ cup all-purpose flour

½ cup cocoa powder

½ cup Ovaltine

2 teaspoons baking powder

½ teaspoon baking soda

1 tablespoon fine sea salt

Coconut & Pecan Frosting (see page 261)

German Chocolate Cake

1. Preheat the oven to 350°F and coat two round 9-inch cake pans with butter.

2. Place the eggs and sugar in the work bowl of a stand mixer fitted with the paddle attachment and beat until pale and fluffy. Add the butter, sour cream, and orange zest and beat until combined.

3. Sift the flours, cocoa powder, Ovaltine, baking powder, baking soda, and salt into a separate bowl. With the mixer running, gradually add the mixture to the work bowl, scraping the sides of the work bowl as needed.

4. Divide the batter between the cake pans and tap them on the counter to distribute the batter evenly and remove any air bubbles. Place the cakes in the oven and bake until a toothpick inserted into their centers comes out clean, 20 to 25 minutes.

5. Remove the cakes from the oven and let them cool in the pans for 10 minutes before transferring them to a wire rack to cool completely.

6. When the cakes have cooled, spread some of the frosting on the top of one cake. Place the other cake on top, spread the remaining frosting over the entire cake, and enjoy.

Yield: 1 Loaf

Active Time: 25 Minutes

Total Time: 6 Hours

INGREDIENTS

¼ teaspoon active dry yeast

¼ teaspoon sugar

1½ cups lukewarm water (90°F)

1 cup semisweet chocolate chips

1 cup unsalted butter, softened, cut into small pieces, plus more as needed

6 egg yolks

1 teaspoon fine sea salt

3 cups all-purpose flour, plus more as needed

1 teaspoon cinnamon

Chocolate & Cinnamon Brioche

1. Place the yeast, sugar, and water in the work bowl of a stand mixer fitted with the dough hook, gently stir, and let the mixture proof until it starts to foam, about 10 minutes.

2. Fill a small saucepan halfway with water and bring it to a simmer. Place the chocolate and butter in a heatproof bowl, place it over the simmering water, and stir until the mixture is melted and smooth. Remove the pan from heat and set it aside.

3. Add the egg yolks to the work bowl of the stand mixer and whisk until scrambled. Add the salt, flour, and cinnamon and work the mixture until it comes together as a sticky dough.

4. Gradually add the chocolate mixture and work the dough until it has been incorporated. Cover the bowl with plastic wrap and let the dough rest for 2 hours.

5. Punch down the dough, cover it, and let it rise for another hour.

6. Coat an 8 x 4–inch loaf pan with butter. Place the dough in the loaf pan and let it rise until it has doubled in size, 1 to 2 hours.

7. Preheat the oven to 450°F. Place the loaf pan in the oven and bake until the brioche is golden brown and sounds hollow when tapped, 35 to 40 minutes.

8. Remove the brioche from the oven and let it cool before removing it from the loaf pan and enjoying.

Chocolate & Cinnamon Brioche

see page 77

INGREDIENTS

12¾ oz. cake flour

1 oz. cocoa powder

½ teaspoon kosher salt

1 teaspoon baking soda

13.4 oz. unsalted butter, softened

14½ oz. sugar

6 eggs

1 teaspoon white vinegar

2½ oz. buttermilk

1 teaspoon pure vanilla extract

2 teaspoons red food coloring

Cream Cheese Frosting (see page 254)

Red Velvet Cake

1. Preheat the oven to 350°F. Line three round 8-inch cake pans with parchment paper and spray with nonstick cooking spray.

2. In a medium bowl, whisk together the cake flour, cocoa powder, salt, and baking soda. Set the mixture aside.

3. In the work bowl of a stand mixer fitted with the paddle attachment, cream the butter and sugar on high speed until the mixture is creamy and fluffy, about 5 minutes. Reduce the speed to low, add the eggs two at a time, and beat until incorporated, scraping down the sides of the bowl with a rubber spatula between additions. Add the vinegar, beat until incorporated, and then add the dry mixture. Beat until thoroughly incorporated, add the buttermilk, vanilla extract, and food coloring, and beat until they have been combined.

4. Pour 1½ cups of batter into each cake pan and bang the pans on the counter to distribute the batter evenly and remove any air bubbles.

5. Place the cakes in the oven and bake until set and cooked through, 26 to 28 minutes. Insert a cake tester in the center of each cake to check for doneness. Remove the cakes from the oven, transfer to a cooling rack, and let them cool completely.

6. Trim a thin layer off the top of each cake to create a flat surface.

7. Place one cake on a cake stand, place 1 cup of the frosting in the center, and level it with an offset spatula. Place the second cake on top and repeat the process with the frosting. Place the last cake on top and spread 2 cups of the frosting over the entire cake, using an offset spatula. Refrigerate the cake for at least 1 hour before slicing and serving.

Yield: 12 Brownies

Active Time: 30 Minutes

Total Time: 3 Hours

INGREDIENTS

7½ oz. dark chocolate (55 to 65 percent)

1½ cups unsalted butter

¾ lb. sugar

¾ lb. light brown sugar

¼ cup plus 1 tablespoon cocoa powder

1 teaspoon kosher salt

5 eggs

1½ tablespoons pure vanilla extract

9½ oz. all-purpose flour

Brownies from Scratch

1. Preheat the oven to 350°F. Line a 13 x 9–inch baking pan with parchment paper and coat it with nonstick cooking spray.

2. Fill a small saucepan halfway with water and bring it to a simmer. Place the dark chocolate and butter in a heatproof bowl, place it over the simmering water, and stir until they have melted and been combined. Remove from heat and set aside.

3. In a separate mixing bowl, whisk the sugar, brown sugar, cocoa powder, and salt together, making sure to break up any clumps. Whisk in the eggs, vanilla, and melted chocolate mixture and then gradually add the flour, whisking to thoroughly incorporate before adding the next bit.

4. Pour the batter into the baking pan and use a rubber spatula to even out the top. Lightly tap the baking pan on the counter to remove any air bubbles.

5. Place the brownies in the oven and bake until a cake tester inserted into the center comes out clean, 30 to 40 minutes.

6. Remove the brownies from the oven, transfer them to a cooling rack, and let them cool completely. Once they are cool, transfer to the refrigerator and chill for 1 hour.

7. Run a paring knife along the sides of the pan, cut the brownies into squares, and enjoy.

Yield: 16 Brownies

Active Time: 15 Minutes

Total Time: 2 Hours

INGREDIENTS

½ lb. unsalted butter, plus more as needed

1¼ cups Guinness

11 oz. sugar-free chocolate chips

3 large eggs

1 teaspoon pure vanilla extract

¾ cup almond flour

1 teaspoon kosher salt

Keto Brownies

1. Preheat the oven to 350°F and coat a square 8-inch baking dish with butter. Place the stout in a medium saucepan, bring it to a boil, and cook until it has reduced by half. Remove the pan from heat and let the stout cool.

2. Place the chocolate chips and butter in a microwave-safe bowl and microwave on medium until melted, removing to stir every 15 seconds.

3. Place the eggs and vanilla in a large mixing bowl and whisk until combined. Slowly whisk in the chocolate-and-butter mixture and then whisk in the reduced stout. Add the almond flour and salt and fold the mixture until it comes together as a smooth batter. Pour the batter into the pan.

4. Place the brownies in the oven and bake until the surface begins to crack and a toothpick inserted into the center comes out with a few moist crumbs attached, about 35 minutes. Remove the brownies from the oven and let them cool in the pan.

5. Cut the brownies into squares and enjoy.

Nutritional Info Per Serving: Calories: 244; Fat: 20.3 g; Net Carbs: 11.8 g; Protein: 2.6 g

Yield: 1 Cake

Active Time: 30 Minutes

Total Time: 2 Hours

INGREDIENTS

4 large eggs, separated

3½ oz. sugar

Zest of 1 lemon

2.8 oz. unsalted butter, melted, plus more as needed

1 oz. amaretto

4.2 oz. semolina flour

3½ oz. blanched almonds, very finely ground

Chocolate Ganache (see page 258), warm

Parrozzo

1. Preheat the oven to 320°F. Place the egg yolks and sugar in a bowl and whisk until the mixture is pale yellow. Add the remaining ingredients, except for the egg whites and ganache, and stir until the mixture comes together as a smooth batter.

2. Place the egg whites in the work bowl of a stand mixer fitted with the whisk attachment and whip until they hold soft peaks. Add the egg whites to the batter and fold to incorporate them.

3. Coat a 6-inch hemisphere pan with butter and pour the batter into it.

4. Place the cake into the oven and bake until a toothpick inserted into the center of it comes out clean, about 20 minutes.

5. Remove the cake from the oven, let it cool for 10 minutes, and then remove it from the pan. Place the cake on a wire rack and let it cool completely.

6. Place a piece of waxed paper beneath the cake on the wire rack and pour the ganache over it.

7. Collect the ganache from the waxed paper and spread it over the cake.

8. Let the ganache set before slicing and serving the cake.

Yield: 1 Cake

Active Time: 30 Minutes

Total Time: 3 Hours

INGREDIENTS

7 oz. unsalted butter, plus more as needed

7 oz. sugar

6 eggs, separated

Zest of 1 orange

2 tablespoons orange liqueur

9 oz. bittersweet chocolate

8.8 oz. almond flour

Confectioners' sugar, for topping

Torta Caprese

1. Preheat the oven to 360°F. Place the butter and sugar in the work bowl of a stand mixer fitted with the paddle attachment and beat the mixture until it is pale and fluffy.

2. Add the egg yolks, orange zest, and liqueur and beat until incorporated.

3. Bring a few inches of water to a simmer in a medium saucepan. Place the chocolate in a heatproof bowl, place it over the simmering water, and stir until it is melted and smooth. Remove the bowl from heat, add the almond flour to the melted chocolate, and stir to combine.

4. Add the butter mixture to the melted chocolate mixture and stir until well combined.

5. Clean out the work bowl of the stand mixer and fit the mixer with the whisk attachment. Place the egg whites in the work bowl and whip until they hold stiff peaks.

6. Add the whipped egg whites to the batter and fold to incorporate.

7. Coat a round 9-inch cake pan with butter, dust it with cocoa powder, and knock out any excess. Pour the batter into the pan, place it in the oven, and bake the cake until a toothpick inserted into the center comes out clean, about 40 minutes.

8. Remove the cake from the oven and let it cool.

9. Dust the cake with confectioners' sugar and enjoy.

Yield: 16 Brownies

Active Time: 15 Minutes

Total Time: 1 Hour and
15 Minutes

INGREDIENTS

**2½ oz. all-purpose flour, plus
more as needed**

4 oz. unsalted butter

4 oz. milk chocolate chips

**3 large eggs, at room
temperature**

7 oz. sugar

Pinch of fine sea salt

1 cup cream cheese, softened

**½ teaspoon pure vanilla
extract**

Marble Brownies

1. Preheat the oven to 350°F. Coat a square 8-inch cake pan with nonstick cooking spray and dust it with flour, knocking out any excess.

2. Fill a small saucepan halfway with water and bring it to a gentle simmer. Place the butter and chocolate chips in a heatproof bowl, place it over the simmering water, and stir until the mixture is melted and smooth. Remove the mixture from heat and let it cool for 5 minutes.

3. Place 2 of the eggs and three-quarters of the sugar in the work bowl of a stand mixer fitted with the paddle attachment and beat on medium speed for 1 minute. Add the chocolate-and-butter mixture, beat for 1 minute, and then add the flour and salt. Beat until just combined, and then pour into the prepared pan.

4. In a separate bowl, combine the cream cheese, remaining sugar, remaining egg, and vanilla. Beat with a handheld mixer on medium speed until light and fluffy. Spread on top of the batter and use a fork to stir the layers together. Place in the oven and bake for 35 minutes, until the top is springy to the touch. Remove, allow the brownies to cool in the pan, and then cut into bars.

Yield: 16 Brownies

Active Time: 15 Minutes

Total Time: 1 Hour and 45 Minutes

INGREDIENTS

12 oz. Guinness or other stout

½ lb. unsalted butter

¾ lb. dark chocolate chips

10½ oz. sugar

3 large eggs

1 teaspoon pure vanilla extract

3¾ oz. all-purpose flour

1¼ teaspoons fine sea salt

Cocoa powder, for topping

Dark Chocolate & Stout Brownies

1. Preheat the oven to 350°F and coat a square 8-inch baking dish with nonstick cooking spray. Place the stout in a medium saucepan and bring to a boil. Cook until it has reduced by half. Remove the pan from heat and let it cool.

2. Fill a small saucepan halfway with water and bring it to a gentle simmer. Place the butter and chocolate chips in a heatproof bowl, place it over the simmering water, and stir until the mixture is melted and smooth. Remove the mixture from heat and let it cool for 5 minutes.

3. Place the sugar, eggs, and vanilla in a large bowl and stir until combined. Slowly whisk in the chocolate-and-butter mixture and then whisk in the stout.

4. Fold in the flour and salt. Pour the batter into the baking dish, place it in the oven, and bake the brownies until the surface begins to crack and a cake tester inserted into the center comes out with a few moist crumbs attached, 35 to 40 minutes.

5. Remove the pan from the oven, place it on a wire rack, and let the brownies cool for 45 minutes.

6. Sprinkle cocoa powder over the top, cut the brownies into squares, and enjoy.

Yield: 12 Brownies

Active Time: 30 Minutes

Total Time: 2 Hours and 45 Minutes

INGREDIENTS

1 lb. dark chocolate (55 to 65 percent)

½ lb. unsalted butter

¾ lb. sugar

4 oz. light brown sugar

¼ cup cocoa powder

¾ teaspoon kosher salt

6 eggs

1½ teaspoons pure vanilla extract

Flourless Fudge Brownies

1. Preheat the oven to 350°F. Line a 13 x 9–inch baking pan with parchment paper and coat it with nonstick cooking spray.

2. Fill a small saucepan halfway with water and bring it to a simmer. Place the dark chocolate and butter in a heatproof bowl, place it over the simmering water, and stir until they have melted and been combined. Remove from heat and set aside.

3. In a separate mixing bowl, whisk the sugar, brown sugar, cocoa powder, and salt together, making sure to break up any clumps. Whisk in the eggs, vanilla, and melted chocolate mixture. Pour the batter into the baking pan and use a rubber spatula to even out the top. Lightly tap the baking pan on the counter to remove any air bubbles.

4. Place the brownies in the oven and bake until a cake tester inserted into the center comes out clean, 30 to 40 minutes.

5. Remove the brownies from the oven, transfer them to a cooling rack, and let them cool completely. Once they are cool, transfer to the refrigerator and chill for 1 hour.

6. Run a paring knife along the sides of the pan, cut the brownies into squares, and enjoy.

Yield: 1 Cake

Active Time: 1 Hour

Total Time: 24 Hours

INGREDIENTS

For the Crust

4 oz. unsalted butter, melted

7 oz. sugar

1½ tablespoons water

⅓ cup cocoa powder

1½ cups all-purpose flour

For the Filling

4½ cups cream cheese, softened

1⅓ cups sugar

4 eggs

2 tablespoons blood orange compound

2 cups sour cream

Chocolate Ganache (see page 258), warm

Blood Orange Cheesecake

1. Preheat the oven to 350°F. To begin preparations for the crust, place the butter and sugar in the work bowl of a stand mixer fitted with the paddle attachment and beat until the mixture is light and fluffy. Add the remaining ingredients and beat until incorporated. Press the mixture into a 9-inch springform pan.

2. Place the pan in the oven and bake for 30 minutes. Remove the crust from the oven and let it cool. Lower the oven temperature to 300°F.

3. Wipe out the work bowl of the stand mixer. To begin preparations for the filling, add the cream cheese and 1 cup of the sugar to the work bowl and beat at medium speed until combined. Incorporate the eggs one at a time, scraping down the work bowl after each has been incorporated. Add the blood orange compound, beat until incorporated, and pour the mixture into the crust.

4. Place the cheesecake in the oven and bake until the edges are set and the center jiggles slightly when you shake the pan, about 1 hour. Turn off the oven, crack the door, and leave the cheesecake in the cooling oven for 1 hour.

5. Remove the cheesecake from the oven. Preheat the oven to 350°F.

6. Place the sour cream and the remaining sugar in a mixing bowl and stir to combine. Spread this mixture over the top of the cheesecake, return it to the oven, and bake it for another 20 minutes.

7. Remove the cheesecake from the oven and let it cool until it is just warm. Cover the cheesecake with plastic wrap and place it in the refrigerator overnight.

8. Spread the ganache over the top of the cheesecake, let the ganache set for 10 minutes, and enjoy.

Yield: 2 Loaves

Active Time: 45 Minutes

Total Time: 4 Hours

INGREDIENTS

For the Filling

6 oz. dark chocolate (55 to 65 percent)

6 oz. unsalted butter

3 oz. confectioners' sugar

2 oz. cocoa powder

For the Dough

1½ cups lukewarm water (90°F)

1 tablespoon plus 2 teaspoons active dry yeast

3 eggs

¼ cup extra-virgin olive oil

2 lbs. bread flour, plus more as needed

¼ cup sugar

1½ tablespoons kosher salt

Chocolate Babka

1. To prepare the filling, fill a small saucepan halfway with water and bring it to a gentle simmer. In a heatproof bowl, combine the dark chocolate and butter. Place the bowl over the simmering water and stir until the mixture is melted and smooth. Remove the bowl from heat, add the confectioners' sugar and cocoa powder, and whisk until thoroughly combined. Set the mixture aside.

2. To begin preparations for the dough, whisk together the water, yeast, eggs, and olive oil in the work bowl of a stand mixer fitted with the dough hook. Add the flour, sugar, and salt and work the mixture on low for 1 minute. Raise the speed to medium and knead the mixture until it comes together as a dough and pulls away from the side of the bowl.

3. Place the dough on a flour-dusted work surface, form it into a ball, and return it to the work bowl. Cover it with plastic wrap and let it rise until doubled in size.

4. Turn the dough out onto a flour-dusted work surface and divide it in half. Use a rolling pin to roll each piece into a 13-inch square.

5. Spread the filling over the pieces of dough, leaving an inch of dough uncovered on the sides closest to yourself. Roll up the pieces of dough and cut them in half lengthwise.

6. With the cut sides facing up, starting from the middle, lift the left half of each piece of dough over the right half, and then lift the right half over the left half. Repeat all the way down to create two-stranded plaits. Tuck the ends of the loaves in.

7. Spray two 8 x 4–inch loaf pans with nonstick cooking spray and place a loaf in each one. Cover the loaves with plastic wrap and let them rise until they crest above the edges of the pans.

8. Preheat the oven to 350°F. Place the loaves in the oven and bake until their internal temperature is 210°F, 45 to 55 minutes.

9. Remove the babka from the oven, place them on a wire rack, and let them cool completely before serving.

Yield: 1 Cake

Active Time: 1 Hour

Total Time: 3 Hours and 30 Minutes

INGREDIENTS

For the Cakes

20 oz. sugar

13 oz. all-purpose flour

4 oz. cocoa powder

1 tablespoon baking soda

1½ teaspoons baking powder

1½ teaspoons kosher salt

1½ cups sour cream

¾ cup canola oil

3 eggs

1½ cups brewed coffee, hot

For the Filling

Butterfluff Filling (see page 255)

¼ cup cocoa powder

For the Frosting

Italian Buttercream (see page 253)

1 cup cocoa powder

Chocolate Ganache (see page 258), warm

Chocolate, shaved, for topping

Triple Chocolate Cake

1. Preheat the oven to 350°F. Line three round 8-inch cake pans with parchment paper and coat them with nonstick cooking spray.

2. To begin preparations for the cakes, sift the sugar, flour, cocoa powder, baking soda, baking powder, and salt into a medium bowl. Set the mixture aside.

3. In the work bowl of a stand mixer fitted with the whisk attachment, combine the sour cream, canola oil, and eggs on medium speed.

4. Reduce the speed to low, add the dry mixture, and whisk until combined. Scrape the sides of the bowl with a rubber spatula as needed. Add the hot coffee and whisk until thoroughly incorporated.

5. Pour 1½ cups of batter into each cake pan. Bang the pans on the countertop to distribute the batter and remove any possible air bubbles.

6. Place the cakes in the oven and bake until a cake tester inserted into the center of each cake comes out clean, 25 to 30 minutes.

7. Remove from the oven and place the cakes on a cooling rack. Let them cool completely.

8. To prepare the filling, place 2 cups of the butterfluff and the cocoa powder in a small bowl and whisk to combine.

9. To prepare the frosting, place the buttercream and cocoa powder in another mixing bowl and whisk until combined. Set the mixtures aside.

10. Trim a thin layer off the top of each cake to create a flat surface. Transfer 2 cups of the frosting to a piping bag and cut a ½-inch slit in it.

11. Place one cake on a cake stand and pipe one ring of frosting around the edge. Place 1 cup of the filling in the center and level it with an offset spatula. Place the second cake on top and repeat the process with the frosting and filling. Place the last cake on top, place 1½ cups of the frosting on the cake, and frost the top and sides of the cake, using an offset spatula. Refrigerate the cake for at least 1 hour.

12. Carefully spoon some the ganache over the edge of the cake, so that it drips down. Spread any remaining ganache over the center of the cake.

13. Place the cake in the refrigerator for 30 minutes so that the ganache hardens. To serve, sprinkle the curls of chocolate over the top and slice.

Yield: 4 Servings

Active Time: 10 Minutes

Total Time: 25 Minutes

INGREDIENTS

Canola oil, as needed

¼ cup heavy cream

4 large eggs

½ teaspoon kosher salt

1 teaspoon baking powder

1 teaspoon pure vanilla extract

½ cup unsweetened cocoa powder

½ cup granulated erythritol or preferred keto-friendly sweetener

Keto Lava Cakes

1. Preheat the oven to 350°F and coat four ramekins with canola oil. Place the cream, eggs, salt, baking powder, and vanilla in a bowl and whisk until combined. Stir in the cocoa powder and erythritol and divide the mixture among 4 ramekins.

2. Place the ramekins in the oven and bake until the cakes are just set, 10 to 12 minutes. Place a plate over the top of each ramekin, invert it, and tap on the counter to release the cake. Enjoy immediately.

Nutritional Info Per Serving: Calories: 152; Fat: 11.8 g; Net Carbs: 3.5 g; Protein: 8.7 g

Yield: 6 Small Cakes

Active Time: 20 Minutes

Total Time: 40 Minutes

INGREDIENTS

1 cup cocoa powder, plus more as needed

3 oz. all-purpose flour

¼ teaspoon kosher salt

½ lb. dark chocolate (55 to 65 percent)

4 oz. unsalted butter

3 eggs

3 egg yolks

4 oz. sugar

Confectioners' sugar, for dusting

Lava Cakes

1. Preheat the oven to 425°F. Spray six 6-oz. ramekins with nonstick cooking spray and coat each one with cocoa powder. Tap out any excess cocoa powder and set the ramekins aside.

2. Sift the flour and salt into a small bowl and set the mixture aside.

3. Fill a small saucepan halfway with water and bring it to a gentle simmer. Place the chocolate and butter in a heatproof mixing bowl and place it over the simmering water. Stir occasionally until the mixture is melted and completely smooth. Remove from heat and set it aside.

4. In another mixing bowl, whisk together the eggs, egg yolks, and sugar. Add the chocolate mixture and whisk until combined. Add the dry mixture and whisk until a smooth batter forms.

5. Pour approximately ½ cup of batter into each of the ramekins. Place them in the oven and bake until the cakes look firm and are crested slightly at the top, 12 to 15 minutes. Remove from the oven and let them cool for 1 minute.

6. Invert each cake onto a plate (be careful, as the ramekins will be very hot). Dust the cakes with confectioners' sugar and serve.

Lava Cakes

see page 103

Yield: 6 Souffles

Active Time: 30 Minutes

Total Time: 1 Hour

INGREDIENTS

9 oz. sugar, plus more as needed

20 oz. dark chocolate (55 to 65 percent)

4 oz. unsalted butter

19 oz. water, plus more as needed

2 oz. heavy cream

11 eggs, separated

1½ oz. sour cream

½ teaspoon cream of tartar

Chocolate Souffles

1. Preheat the oven to 375°F. Coat the insides of six 8-oz. ramekins with nonstick cooking spray. Place 2 tablespoons of sugar in each ramekin and spread it to evenly coat the insides of the dishes. Knock out any excess sugar and set the ramekins aside.

2. Place the dark chocolate and butter in a large, heatproof bowl. Add 2 inches of water to a small saucepan and bring it to a simmer. Place the bowl on top and melt the butter and chocolate together over the double boiler.

3. In a medium saucepan, bring the water and heavy cream to a simmer. Remove the chocolate mixture from the double boiler and whisk it into the water-and-cream mixture. Remove the saucepan from heat.

4. Place the egg yolks and sour cream in a mixing bowl and whisk until combined. Gradually incorporate the cream-and-chocolate mixture, while whisking constantly. Set the mixture aside.

5. In the work bowl of a stand mixer fitted with the whisk attachment, whip the egg whites and cream of tartar on high until the mixture holds stiff peaks. Reduce the speed to medium and gradually incorporate the 9 oz. of sugar. Once all of the sugar has been incorporated, raise the speed back to high and whip until it is a glossy, stiff meringue.

6. Working in three increments, add the meringue to the chocolate base, folding gently with a rubber spatula.

7. Spoon the souffle base to the rims of the ramekins. Gently tap the bottoms of the ramekins with the palm of your hand to remove any air, but not so hard as to deflate the meringue.

8. Place in the oven and bake until the souffles have risen significantly and set on the outside, but are still jiggly at the center, 25 to 27 minutes. Remove from the oven and serve immediately.

Yield: 1 Cake

Active Time: 3 Hours

Total Time: 15 Hours

INGREDIENTS

For the Cake

1 oz. all-purpose flour

1 tablespoon cocoa powder

2 oz. almond flour

2.4 oz. confectioners' sugar

3 egg whites

¼ teaspoon kosher salt

2 tablespoons sugar

For the Gelee

2 sheets of silver gelatin

¼ cup water

7 oz. passion fruit puree

3 tablespoons sugar

For the Mousse

2 sheets of silver gelatin

1 lb. dark chocolate (55 to 65 percent)

14 oz. plus ½ cup heavy cream

½ cup milk

2 egg yolks

2 tablespoons sugar

For the Glaze

5 sheets of silver gelatin

9 oz. sugar

5 oz. water

3 oz. cocoa powder

3 oz. sour cream

2 oz. dark chocolate

Dark Chocolate Entremet

1. Preheat the oven to 350°F. Coat a round 6-inch cake pan with nonstick cooking spray.

2. To begin preparations for the cake, sift the flour, cocoa powder, almond flour, and confectioners' sugar into a medium bowl. Set the mixture aside.

3. In the work bowl of a stand mixer fitted with the whisk attachment, whip the egg whites and salt on high until soft peaks begin to form. Reduce the speed to low and gradually incorporate the sugar. Raise the speed to high and whip the mixture until it holds stiff peaks.

4. Fold the meringue into the dry mixture until fully incorporated and then pour the batter into the prepared cake pan.

5. Place the cake in the oven and bake until set and a cake tester comes out clean after being inserted, 10 to 12 minutes. Remove the cake from the oven and set it on a wire rack to cool completely. Once cool, remove the cake from the pan and set aside.

6. To begin preparations for the gelee, place the gelatin sheets in a small bowl, and add 1 cup of ice and enough cold water to cover the sheets. Place the water, passion fruit puree, and sugar in a small saucepan and bring to a simmer over medium heat.

7. Prepare a 6-inch ring mold by wrapping plastic wrap tightly over the bottom. Set the ring mold on a small baking sheet.

8. Remove the pan from heat. Remove the gelatin from the ice bath and squeeze out as much water as possible. Whisk the gelatin into the passion fruit mixture until fully dissolved. Let the gelee cool to room temperature and then pour it into the ring mold. Place the cake ring in the freezer for at least 4 hours to fully freeze.

9. To begin preparations for the mousse, place the gelatin sheets in a small bowl, and add 1 cup of ice and enough cold water to cover the sheets.

10. Prepare an 8-inch ring mold by wrapping plastic wrap tightly over the bottom. Set the ring mold on a small baking sheet.

11. Fill a small saucepan halfway with water and bring it to a gentle simmer. Place the dark chocolate in a heatproof bowl, place the bowl over the simmering water, and stir with a rubber spatula until the chocolate has melted. Remove the chocolate from heat and set it aside.

12. In the work bowl of a stand mixer fitted with the whisk attachment, whip 14 oz. of the heavy cream on high until soft peaks form. Place the whipped cream in the refrigerator.

13. In a small saucepan, combine the milk and remaining heavy cream and bring to a boil over medium heat.

14. Place the egg yolks and sugar in a small bowl and whisk to combine. Gradually add the heated milk mixture into the egg-and-sugar mixture, while whisking constantly. When fully incorporated, transfer the tempered mixture back into the saucepan.

15. Cook the mixture over medium heat, whisking until the mixture has thickened slightly and reads 175°F on an instant-read thermometer. Remove the pan from heat, remove the gelatin from the ice bath, and squeeze out as much water as possible. Whisk the gelatin into the warm mousse until fully dissolved.

16. Pour the mixture over the melted chocolate and stir to combine.

17. Remove the whipped cream from the refrigerator and, working in two increments, fold it into the mixture.

18. Pour 2 cups of the mousse into the 8-inch ring mold. Spread it into an even layer with an offset spatula.

19. Remove the passion fruit gelee from the freezer, carefully remove the plastic wrap, and remove the gelee from the cake ring. Place the gelee in the center of the mousse and press down.

20. Add more of the mousse until it reaches about ½ inch from the top of the ring mold.

21. Place the chocolate cake in the mousse, top side down, and push down gently until the cake and mousse are level with each other.

22. Transfer the entremet to the freezer and chill for at least 4 hours.

23. To begin preparations for the glaze, place the gelatin sheets in a small bowl, and add 1 cup of ice and enough cold water to cover the sheets.

24. In a medium saucepan, combine the sugar, water, cocoa powder, and sour cream and warm over low heat, stirring continuously until the mixture begins to steam. Take care to not let the mixture come to a boil, as it can burn easily.

25. Remove the pan from heat, remove the gelatin from the ice bath, and squeeze out as much water as possible. Whisk the gelatin into the warm mixture until fully dissolved.

26. Add the dark chocolate and stir until the mixture is smooth. Let the glaze cool to 95°F.

27. Remove the entremet from the freezer and peel off the plastic wrap from the bottom. Using a kitchen torch, lightly heat the sides of the ring mold to loosen the entremet.

28. Place a wire rack on a piece of parchment paper. Flip the entremet over so that the cake is bottom side up.

29. Pour the glaze carefully and evenly over the top in a circular motion, starting from the center and working out toward the edge. Allow the glaze to fall over the side and cover the entirety of the cake. Use an offset spatula to spread the glaze as needed. If there are any air bubbles, carefully go over them with a kitchen torch, as a smooth, shiny finish is a key piece of a successful entremet.

30. Using a spatula, transfer the glazed cake to a serving tray and refrigerate for 4 hours, to allow the glaze to set and the center of the cake to thaw. When ready to serve, use a hot knife to cut the cake.

Dark Chocolate Entremet
see pages 108-109

Yield: 1 Cake

Active Time: 1 Hour

Total Time: 3 Hours and 30 Minutes

INGREDIENTS

20 oz. sugar

13 oz. all-purpose flour

4 oz. cocoa powder

1 tablespoon baking soda

1½ teaspoons baking powder

1½ teaspoons kosher salt

1½ cups sour cream

¾ cup canola oil

3 eggs

1½ cups brewed coffee, hot

2 batches of Whipped Cream (see page 255)

2 cups cherry jam

Chocolate Ganache (see page 258), made with dark chocolate, warm

Dark chocolate, shaved, for garnish

2 cups fresh red cherries, for garnish

Black Forest Cake

1. Preheat the oven to 350°F. Line three round 8-inch cake pans with parchment paper and coat them with nonstick cooking spray.

2. In a medium bowl, sift the sugar, flour, cocoa powder, baking soda, baking powder, and salt into a mixing bowl and set it aside.

3. In the work bowl of a stand mixer fitted with the whisk attachment, combine the sour cream, canola oil, and eggs on medium speed. Reduce the speed to low, add the dry mixture, and beat until combined. Scrape the sides of the work bowl with a rubber spatula as needed.

4. With the mixer running on low, gradually add the hot coffee and beat until fully incorporated. Pour 1½ cups of batter into each cake pan. Bang the pans on the counter to distribute the batter evenly and remove any air bubbles.

5. Place the cakes in the oven and bake until browned and cooked through, 25 to 30 minutes. Insert a cake tester into the center of each cake to check for doneness. Remove the cakes from the oven, transfer them to a cooling rack, and let them cool completely.

6. Trim a thin layer off the top of each cake to create a flat surface. Transfer 2 cups of the Whipped Cream into a piping bag and cut a ½-inch slit in the bag.

7. Place one cake on a cake stand and pipe one ring of cream around the edge. Place 1 cup of the cherry jam in the center and level it with an offset spatula. Place the second cake on top and repeat the process with the Whipped Cream and cherry jam. Place the last cake on top and spread 1½ cups of the Whipped Cream over the entire cake, using an offset spatula. Refrigerate the cake for at least 1 hour.

8. Carefully spoon some the ganache over the edge of the cake, so that it drips down. Spread any remaining ganache over the center of the cake.

9. Place the cake in the refrigerator for 30 minutes, so that the ganache hardens.

10. Garnish the cake with the shaved chocolate and fresh cherries before slicing and serving.

Yield: 1 Cake

Active Time: 45 Minutes

Total Time: 3 Hours and 15 Minutes

INGREDIENTS

2 medium red beets, rinsed

4½ oz. all-purpose flour

3 tablespoons cocoa powder

1¼ teaspoons baking powder

¼ teaspoon kosher salt

7 oz. dark chocolate (55 to 65 percent)

7 oz. unsalted butter

¼ cup milk

5 eggs

7 oz. sugar

1 Cup Chocolate Ganache (see page 258), warm

Fresh blackberries, for garnish

Chocolate Beet Cake

1. Preheat the oven to 350°F. Coat a round 9-inch cake pan with nonstick cooking spray.

2. Place the beets in a large saucepan, cover them with water, and bring it to a boil. Cook the beets until they are very tender when poked with a knife, about 1 hour. Drain and let the beets cool. When cool enough to handle, rinse the beets under cold water and rub off their skins. Cut the beets into 1-inch chunks, place them in a food processor, and puree. Set the beets aside.

3. Whisk the flour, cocoa powder, baking powder, and salt together in a small bowl. Set the mixture aside.

4. Bring a small saucepan filled halfway with water to a gentle simmer. Add the chocolate and butter to a heatproof mixing bowl and set it over the simmering water until it melts, stirring occasionally. Remove from heat and set the mixture aside.

5. Place the milk in a clean saucepan, warm it over medium-low heat until it starts to steam, and pour it into the chocolate mixture. Stir to combine, add the eggs and sugar, and whisk until incorporated. Add the beet puree, stir to incorporate, and add the dry mixture. Whisk until the mixture comes together as a smooth batter.

6. Pour the batter into the prepared cake pan, place it in the oven, and bake until baked through, 40 to 45 minutes. Insert a cake tester into the center of the cake to check for doneness. Remove from the oven, transfer the cake to a cooling rack, and let it cool completely.

7. Carefully remove the cake from the pan and transfer to a serving plate.

8. Spread the warm ganache over the top of the cake, garnish with blackberries, and serve.

Yield: 24 Cupcakes

Active Time: 40 Minutes

Total Time: 2 Hours

INGREDIENTS

20 oz. sugar

13 oz. all-purpose flour

4 oz. cocoa powder

1 tablespoon baking soda

1½ teaspoons baking powder

1½ teaspoons kosher salt

1½ cups sour cream

¾ cup canola oil

3 eggs

1½ cups brewed coffee, hot

Butterfluff Filling
(see page 255)

Chocolate Ganache
(see page 258), warm

Chocolate Cupcakes

1. Preheat the oven to 350°F. Line a 24-well cupcake pan with liners.

2. In a medium bowl, whisk together the sugar, flour, cocoa powder, baking soda, baking powder, and salt. Sift the mixture into a separate bowl and set it aside.

3. In the work bowl of a stand mixer fitted with the whisk attachment, combine the sour cream, canola oil, and eggs on medium speed.

4. Reduce the speed to low, add the dry mixture, and beat until incorporated, scraping the sides of the bowl with a rubber spatula as needed. Gradually add the hot coffee and beat until thoroughly incorporated. Pour about ¼ cup of batter into each cupcake liner.

5. Place the cupcakes in the oven and bake until a cake tester inserted into the center of each cupcake comes out clean, 18 to 22 minutes. Remove the cupcakes from the oven and place them on a wire rack until completely cool.

6. Using a cupcake corer or a sharp paring knife, carefully remove the center of each cupcake. Place 2 cups of the Butterfluff Filling in a piping bag and fill the centers of the cupcakes with it.

7. While the ganache is warm, dip the tops of the cupcakes in the ganache and place them on a flat baking sheet. Refrigerate the cupcakes for 20 minutes so that the chocolate will set.

8. Place 1 cup of the Butterfluff Filling in a piping bag fit with a thin, plain tip and pipe decorative curls on top of each cupcake. Allow the curls to set for 10 minutes before serving.

Yield: 1 Cheesecake

Active Time: 30 Minutes

Total Time: 8 Hours

For the Crust

24 Oreo cookies

3 oz. unsalted butter, melted

For the Filling

15 Oreo cookies

2 lbs. cream cheese, softened

⅔ cup sugar

¼ teaspoon kosher salt

4 eggs

1 teaspoon pure vanilla extract

Whipped Cream (see page 255), for serving

Cookies 'N' Cream Cheesecake

1. Preheat the oven to 350°F. To begin preparations for the crust, place the cookies in a food processor and pulse until finely ground. Transfer to a medium bowl and combine with the melted butter.

2. Transfer the mixture to a 9-inch pie plate and press it into the bottom and side in an even layer. Use the bottom of a dry measuring cup to help flatten the bottom of the crust. Use a paring knife to trim away any excess crust and create a flat and smooth edge.

3. Place the pie plate on a baking sheet and bake until it is firm, 8 to 10 minutes. Remove from the oven, transfer the crust to a cooling rack, and let it cool for at least 2 hours.

4. Preheat the oven to 350°F. To begin preparations for the filling, place the cookies in a food processor and pulse until finely ground. Set them aside.

5. Bring 8 cups of water to a boil in a small saucepan.

6. In the work bowl of a stand mixer fitted with the paddle attachment, cream the cream cheese, sugar, and salt on high until the mixture is fluffy, about 10 minutes. Scrape down the sides of the work bowl as needed.

7. Reduce the speed of the mixer to medium and incorporate one egg at a time, scraping down the work bowl as needed. Add the vanilla and beat until incorporated. Remove the work bowl from the mixer and fold in the cookie crumbs.

8. Pour the mixture into the crust, place the cheesecake in a large baking pan with high sides, and gently pour the boiling water into the baking pan until it reaches halfway up the sides of the pie plate.

9. Cover the baking pan with aluminum foil, place it in the oven, and bake until the cheesecake is set and only slightly jiggly in the center, 50 minutes to 1 hour. Turn off the oven and leave the oven door cracked. Allow the cheesecake to rest in the cooling oven for 45 minutes.

10. Remove the cheesecake from the oven and transfer it to a cooling rack. Let it sit at room temperature for 1 hour. Refrigerate the cheesecake for at least 4 hours before serving and slicing. To serve, top each slice with a heaping spoonful of Whipped Cream.

Yield: 1 Cake

Active Time: 30 Minutes

Total Time: 3 Hours and 30 Minutes

INGREDIENTS

9 oz. dark chocolate (55 to 65 percent)

4 oz. unsalted butter

¼ cup water, plus more as needed

Pinch of kosher salt

3 oz. sugar

3 eggs

½ teaspoon pure vanilla extract

Confectioners' sugar, for dusting

Fresh raspberries, for garnish

Flourless Chocolate Torte

1. Preheat the oven to 375°F. Line a round 9-inch cake pan with parchment paper and coat it with nonstick cooking spray.

2. Fill a small saucepan halfway with water and bring it to a gentle simmer. In a heatproof medium bowl, combine the chocolate and butter. Place the bowl over the simmering water and stir the mixture with a rubber spatula until it has melted. Remove the mixture from heat and set it aside.

3. In another small saucepan, bring the water, salt, and sugar to a boil over medium heat. Pour the mixture into the melted chocolate and whisk to combine. Incorporate the eggs and vanilla and then pour the batter into the prepared cake pan.

4. Place the cake in the oven and bake until set and the internal temperature reaches 200°F, 25 to 30 minutes. Remove the cake from the oven and let it cool on a wire rack for 30 minutes.

5. Place the torte in the refrigerator for 2 hours.

6. Run a paring knife along the edge of the pan and invert the torte onto a serving plate. Dust the top of the torte with confectioners' sugar and garnish with fresh raspberries.

Flourless Chocolate Torte

see page 119

Yield: 1 Cake

Active Time: 3 Hours

Total Time: 3 Hours and 45 Minutes

INGREDIENTS

For the Joconde

5 oz. fine almond flour

5 oz. confectioners' sugar

1 oz. all-purpose flour

5 eggs

5 egg whites

¼ teaspoon kosher salt

2 tablespoons sugar

For the Coffee Syrup

½ cup water

½ cup sugar

1 tablespoon ground espresso

For the Hazelnut & Praline Crunch

4 oz. dark chocolate (55 to 65 percent)

4 oz. praline paste

3 oz. feuilletine flakes

For the Mocha Cream

1 cup sugar

¼ cup water

6 egg yolks

3 tablespoons espresso powder

½ lb. unsalted butter, softened

Chocolate Ganache (see page 258), at room temperature, for topping

Opera Torte

1. Preheat the oven to 400°F. Coat two 13 x 9–inch baking pans with nonstick cooking spray.

2. To begin preparations for the joconde, sift the almond flour, confectioners' sugar, and all-purpose flour into a large bowl. Add the eggs and whisk until combined. Set the mixture aside.

3. In the work bowl of a stand mixer fitted with the whisk attachment, whip the egg whites and salt on high until soft peaks begin to form. Reduce the speed to low and gradually incorporate the sugar. Raise the speed back to high and continue to whip until stiff peaks form. Add the meringue to the dry mixture and fold until thoroughly incorporated. Divide the batter between the two prepared pans, place them in the oven, and bake until they are set and lightly browned, 8 to 10 minutes. Remove from the oven, transfer to a cooling rack, and let them cool completely.

4. To prepare the coffee syrup, place the water, sugar, and espresso in a small saucepan and bring to a simmer over medium heat, while stirring frequently to dissolve the sugar and espresso. Remove from heat and let the syrup cool completely.

5. To prepare the hazelnut and praline crunch, bring a small saucepan filled halfway with water to a gentle simmer. Place the chocolate in a small heatproof bowl, place it over the simmering water, and stir until the chocolate has melted. Remove the bowl from heat, stir in the praline paste and the feuilletine flakes, and spread the mixture over the two joconde. Place the cakes in the refrigerator.

6. To begin preparations for the mocha cream, place the sugar and water in a small saucepan over high heat. Cook until the mixture reaches 245°F on a candy thermometer.

7. While the sugar and water are heating up, place the egg yolks and espresso powder in the work bowl of a stand mixer fitted with the whisk attachment and whip the mixture on high.

8. When the syrup reaches the correct temperature, gradually add it to the egg yolk mixture. Continue to whip on high until the mixture cools slightly. Reduce the speed to low and gradually add the softened butter. When all of the butter has been incorporated, raise the speed back to high and whip the mixture until smooth and fluffy. Set the mocha cream aside.

9. Remove both cakes from the refrigerator and carefully remove them from the pans. Place one cake on a serving tray with the coated layer facing down. Brush the cake with some of the coffee syrup and spread half of the mocha cream over the top. Lay the second cake on top so that the mocha and hazelnut layers are touching. Brush the top of this cake with the remaining coffee syrup and then spread the remaining mocha cream over the cake.

10. Place the cake in the refrigerator for 30 minutes. Spread the Chocolate Ganache over the entire cake and let it sit for 10 minutes. To serve, use a hot knife to cut the cake into rectangles.

Note: Feuilletine flakes are a crispy confection made from thin, sweetened crepes. They can be found at many baking shops, and are also available online.

Opera Torte
see pages 122-123

Yield: 10 to 12 Servings

Active Time: 45 Minutes

Total Time: 3 Hours

INGREDIENTS

7½ oz. all-purpose flour

1.8 oz. cocoa powder, plus more as needed

¾ lb. sugar

1½ teaspoons kosher salt

¾ teaspoon baking powder

5 oz. canola oil

5 eggs

5 oz. water

7 egg whites

½ teaspoon cream of tartar

Butterfluff Filling (see page 255)

Chocolate Ganache (see page 258), warm

Chocolate Cake Roll

1. Preheat the oven to 350°F. Line an 18 x 13–inch baking sheet with parchment paper and coat it with nonstick cooking spray.

2. Sift the flour, cocoa powder, 7 oz. of the sugar, the salt, and baking powder into a small bowl. Set the mixture aside.

3. In a medium bowl, whisk the canola oil, eggs, and water until combined. Add the dry mixture and whisk until combined.

4. In the work bowl of a stand mixer fitted with the whisk attachment, whip the egg whites and cream of tartar on high until soft peaks begin to form. Reduce the speed to low and add the remaining sugar a few tablespoons at a time. When all of the sugar has been incorporated, raise the speed back to high and whip until the mixture holds stiff peaks.

5. Remove the work bowl from the mixer. Gently fold half of the meringue into the cake batter. Add the remaining meringue and fold until no white streaks remain. Spread the cake batter over the baking sheet, place it in the oven, and bake until the center of the cake springs back when poked with a finger and a cake tester comes out clean, 10 to 12 minutes. Remove the cake from the oven and immediately dust the top with cocoa powder. Turn the sponge cake onto a fresh piece of parchment paper. Peel the parchment away from the bottom side of the cake. Place a fresh piece of parchment on the bottom of the cake and turn it over so that the dusted side of the cake is facing up.

6. Using a rolling pin, gently roll up the cake tightly, starting from a short end. Let the cake cool to room temperature while coiled around the rolling pin.

7. Gently unroll the cake and spread the filling evenly over the top, leaving an approximately ½-inch border around the edges. Carefully roll the cake back up with your hands (do not use the rolling pin). Place the cake roll on a cooling rack that has parchment paper beneath it.

8. Pour the ganache over the cake roll. Refrigerate for at least 1 hour to let the chocolate set before slicing and serving.

PIES, TARTS & PASTRIES

With so many wonderful options available, pies and pastries may not be the first treats that come to mind when you're looking for a chocolate fix. But if you think back to those desserts that were the best you ever had, combining aesthetics, flavor, and mouth-feel into something approaching perfection, it's likely to have been one of the desserts here, be it a luscious slice of chocolate cream pie, an irresistible eclair, or a decadent cannoli.

Yield: 1 Pie

Active Time: 10 Minutes

Total Time: 2 Hours and 15 Minutes

INGREDIENTS

2 cups semisweet chocolate chips

2½ cups heavy cream

1 tablespoon bourbon

1 teaspoon pure vanilla extract

1 Graham Cracker Crust (see page 251)

Chocolate Mousse Pie

1. Preheat the oven to 350°F. Bring a few inches of water to a simmer in a medium saucepan. Place the chocolate and ½ cup of cream in a heatproof bowl, place it over the simmering water, and stir until the mixture is melted and smooth.

2. Stir in the bourbon and vanilla and let the mixture stand for about 5 minutes.

3. Place the remaining cream in the work bowl of a stand mixer fitted with the whisk attachment and whisk at medium-high speed until medium peaks form.

4. Add the chocolate mixture to the whipped cream and fold until combined. Spoon the filling into the piecrust and smooth the top with a rubber spatula.

5. Place the pie in the refrigerator and chill for at least 2 hours before serving.

Yield: 3 Servings

Active Time: 5 Minutes

Total Time: 1 Hour and 45 Minutes

INGREDIENTS

1½ oz. almond flour

1 teaspoon unsweetened cocoa powder

Stevia or preferred keto-friendly sweetener, to taste

1 teaspoon pure vanilla extract

2 tablespoons salted butter, melted

1 teaspoon instant espresso powder

2 tablespoons hot water (125°F)

5.3 oz. mascarpone cheese

3½ oz. heavy cream

1 oz. dark chocolate (85 percent)

Coarse sea salt, for topping

Keto Coffee & Chocolate Tarts

1. Preheat the oven to 350°F. Place the almond flour, cocoa powder, sweetener, vanilla, and butter in a mixing bowl and stir until the mixture has the consistency of wet sand.

2. Divide the mixture among three ramekins and press it into their bases until it is smooth and even. Place the ramekins in the oven and bake the bases for 10 minutes. Remove the bases from the oven and let them cool slightly.

3. Dissolve the instant espresso powder in the hot water and let it cool.

4. Place the mascarpone cheese, more sweetener, and the espresso in a bowl and beat until the mixture is light and fluffy. Pour the mascarpone mixture over the cooled tart bases and refrigerate the tarts for 10 minutes.

5. Place the heavy cream in a microwave-safe bowl and microwave on medium for 30 seconds. Add the chocolate and more sweetener and stir until you have a creamy ganache. Pour the ganache over the tarts and refrigerate for 1 hour.

6. Sprinkle sea salt over the tarts and enjoy.

Nutritional Info Per Serving: Calories: 490; Fat: 49 g; Net Carbs: 3 g; Protein: 8 g

Yield: 1 Pie

Active Time: 20 Minutes

Total Time: 2 Hours and 15 Minutes

INGREDIENTS

6 cups peeled and chopped carrots

4 tablespoons unsalted butter, divided into tablespoons

2 teaspoons pure vanilla extract

¾ cup white chocolate chips

2 teaspoons ground ginger

1 large egg

3 large egg yolks

1¼ cups packed light brown sugar

1¼ cups sour cream

1 Graham Cracker Crust (see page 251)

Carrot & White Chocolate Pie

1. Preheat the oven to 400°F. Place the carrots, butter, and vanilla in a large mixing bowl and stir to combine. Place the mixture on a large, rimmed baking sheet and roast, removing to toss two or three times, until the carrots are fork-tender, about 1 hour.

2. Remove the baking sheet from the oven and place the carrots in a food processor. Pulse until minced, add the white chocolate chips, and pulse until they have melted. Add the ginger, egg, egg yolks, light brown sugar, and sour cream and puree until smooth, scraping down the work bowl as needed. Reduce the oven's temperature to 325°F.

3. Evenly distribute the filling in the piecrust, place the pie in the oven, and bake for about 50 minutes, until the filling is set and dry to the touch. Remove from the oven and let cool before enjoying.

Yield: 1 Pie

Active Time: 45 Minutes

Total Time: 2 Hours and 30 Minutes

INGREDIENTS

6½ oz. all-purpose flour

1½ teaspoons baking powder

½ teaspoon kosher salt

3 eggs

½ lb. sugar

½ cup milk

3 oz. unsalted butter

2 teaspoons pure vanilla extract

Pastry Cream (see page 254)

½ cup heavy cream

1 tablespoon light corn syrup

4 oz. dark chocolate (55 to 65 percent)

Boston Cream Pie

1. Preheat the oven to 350°F. Line two round 9-inch cake pans with parchment paper and coat them with nonstick cooking spray.

2. Sift the flour, baking powder, and salt into a bowl. Set the mixture aside.

3. In the work bowl of a stand mixer fitted with the whisk attachment, whip the eggs and sugar on high until the mixture is pale and thick, about 5 minutes.

4. Reduce the speed to low, add the dry mixture, and beat until incorporated.

5. Combine the milk and butter in a small saucepan and warm over medium heat until the butter has melted. Whisk in the vanilla and remove the pan from heat. With the mixer running on low, add the milk mixture to the work bowl and beat the mixture until it comes together as a smooth batter.

6. Divide the batter between the cake pans. Bang the pans on the countertop to spread the batter and remove any possible air bubbles.

7. Place the cakes in the oven and bake until they are lightly golden brown and baked through, 35 to 40 minutes. Insert a cake tester into the center of each cake to check for doneness.

8. Remove the cakes from the oven and place them on a cooling rack. Let them cool completely.

9. Trim a thin layer off the top of each cake to create a flat surface Place one cake on a cake stand. Place 1 cup of the Pastry Cream in the center and spread it with an offset spatula. Place the second cake on top.

10. Combine the heavy cream and corn syrup in a saucepan and bring it to a boil, stirring to dissolve the corn syrup. Remove the pan from heat and add the dark chocolate. Stir until the chocolate has melted and the mixture is smooth. Let the ganache cool for 10 minutes.

11. Pour the ganache over the cake and spread it to the edge, allowing some ganache to drip down the side. Let the cake rest for 20 minutes before slicing.

Boston Cream Pie

see page 135

Yield: 20 Whoopie Pies

Active Time: 30 Minutes

Total Time: 1 Hour

INGREDIENTS

9 oz. all-purpose flour

1½ oz. cocoa powder

1½ teaspoons baking soda

½ teaspoon kosher salt

4 oz. unsalted butter, softened

½ lb. sugar

1 egg

1 teaspoon pure vanilla extract

1 cup buttermilk

2 cups Butterfluff Filling (see page 255)

Whoopie Pies

1. Preheat the oven to 350°F and line two baking sheets with parchment paper. Sift the flour, cocoa powder, baking soda, and salt into a mixing bowl. Set the mixture aside.

2. In the work bowl of a stand mixer fitted with the paddle attachment, cream the butter and sugar on medium until the mixture is very light and fluffy, about 5 minutes. Scrape down the work bowl with a rubber spatula and then beat the mixture for another 5 minutes.

3. Reduce the speed to low, add the egg, and beat until incorporated. Scrape down the work bowl, raise the speed to medium, and beat the mixture for 1 minute.

4. Reduce the speed to low, add the vanilla and the dry mixture, and beat until it comes together as a smooth batter. Add the buttermilk in a slow stream and beat to incorporate.

5. Scoop 2-oz. portions of the batter onto the baking sheets, making sure to leave 2 inches between each portion. Tap the bottom of the baking sheets gently on the counter to remove any air bubbles and let the portions spread out slightly.

6. Place in the oven and bake until a cake tester inserted into the centers of the whoopie pies comes out clean, 10 to 12 minutes.

7. Remove the whoopie pies from the oven and let them cool completely on the baking sheets.

8. Carefully remove the whoopie pies from the parchment paper. Scoop about 2 oz. of the Butterfluff Filling on half of the whoopie pies and then create sandwiches by topping with the remaining half.

Yield: 1 Pie

Active Time: 15 Minutes

Total Time: 1 Hour and 30 Minutes

INGREDIENTS

¾ lb. white chocolate chips

4 oz. unsalted butter, cut into small pieces

2 eggs

1 cup heavy cream

½ cup sugar

1 teaspoon pure vanilla extract

Pinch of fine sea salt

1 Pâté Sucrée (see page 252), blind baked

White chocolate, shaved, for topping

¼ cup hulled and sliced strawberries, for topping

White Chocolate Pie

1. Preheat the oven to 350°F. Fill a small saucepan halfway with water and bring it to a simmer. Place the white chocolate chips and butter in a large heatproof bowl, place it over the simmering water, and stir occasionally until the mixture is melted and combined. Remove from heat and set it aside.

2. In a mixing bowl, whisk together the eggs, cream, sugar, vanilla, and salt. While whisking constantly, gradually add the white chocolate mixture. Pour the filling into the crust and gently tap the pie plate to evenly distribute the filling.

3. Place the pie in the oven and bake until the filling is set around the edges but still soft in the center, 15 to 20 minutes. Remove from the oven and let cool completely before topping with the white chocolate shavings and strawberries.

Yield: 1 Pie

Active Time: 30 Minutes

Total Time: 3 Hours

INGREDIENTS

1 Perfect Piecrust (see page 251), rolled out

½ lb. large pecan halves

3 eggs

6 oz. dark brown sugar

1 cup light corn syrup

1 teaspoon pure vanilla extract

½ teaspoon kosher salt

2 tablespoons bourbon

5 oz. semisweet chocolate chips

Chocolate & Bourbon Pecan Pie

1. Preheat the oven to 375°F. Coat a 9-inch pie plate with nonstick cooking spray and place the piecrust in it. Trim away any excess and crimp the edge.

2. Place the pecans on a parchment-lined baking sheet, place them in the oven, and toast until fragrant, 8 to 10 minutes. Remove the pecans from the oven and let them cool.

3. Place the eggs, dark brown sugar, corn syrup, vanilla, salt, and bourbon in a mixing bowl and whisk until combined.

4. Cover the bottom of the piecrust with the semisweet chocolate chips. Arrange the toasted pecans on top of the chocolate chips and then pour the filling into the crust.

5. Place the pie in the oven and bake until the center of the pie is set, 55 to 60 minutes.

6. Remove the pie from the oven, place it on a cooling rack, and let it cool for 1 to 2 hours before slicing and serving.

Yield: 1 Pie

Active Time: 15 Minutes

Total Time: 1 Hour and 45 Minutes

INGREDIENTS

6 oz. unsalted butter

1 cup packed dark brown sugar

4 large eggs, lightly beaten

¼ cup cocoa powder

1¼ cups bittersweet chocolate chips, melted and slightly cooled

2 teaspoons espresso powder

1¼ cups heavy cream

1 Cocoa Crust (see page 252)

Whipped Cream (see page 255), for topping

Dark chocolate, shaved, for topping

Mississippi Mud Pie

1. Preheat the oven to 350°F. Place the butter and brown sugar in the work bowl of a stand mixer fitted with the paddle attachment and beat on medium until pale and fluffy, about 5 minutes. Add the eggs and cocoa powder, beat to incorporate, and then fold in the chocolate chips and espresso powder. Add the cream and beat until incorporated.

2. Evenly distribute the mixture in the piecrust, place the pie in the oven, and bake until the filling is set, about 35 minutes. Remove from the oven and let the pie cool completely. Top with the Whipped Cream and shaved chocolate before serving.

Yield: 1 Pie

Active Time: 10 Minutes

Total Time: 1 Hour and 10 Minutes

INGREDIENTS

6 cups Chocolate Pudding (see page 179)

1 Perfect Piecrust (see page 251), blind baked

2 cups Whipped Cream (see page 255)

Chocolate shavings, raspberries, or sliced strawberries, for garnish

Chocolate Cream Pie

1. Place the pudding in the piecrust, smooth the top with a rubber spatula, and cover with plastic wrap. Refrigerate for 1 hour.

2. When ready to serve, spread the Whipped Cream on top of the filling in a thick layer. Garnish with the chocolate shavings, raspberries, or strawberries, if desired.

INGREDIENTS

For the Crust

10 oz. cake flour

½ teaspoon fine sea salt

2 oz. unsalted butter, frozen and grated

2.1 oz. lard

¼ cup ice water

1 tablespoon heavy cream

1 egg yolk

For the Filling

5 tablespoons cake flour

½ cup sifted cocoa powder

⅛ teaspoon fine sea salt

1 lb. sugar

¾ cup water

5 large egg yolks

1¾ cups evaporated milk

2½ teaspoons pure vanilla extract

1¼ oz. unsalted butter, cut into small pieces

For the Meringue

1½ egg whites, at room temperature

½ teaspoon cream of tartar

8¾ oz. sugar

Chocolate Meringue Pie

1. Coat a 9-inch pie plate with nonstick cooking spray and preheat the oven to 375°F. To begin preparations for the crust, combine the flour, salt, butter, and lard in a mixing bowl and work the mixture with a pastry cutter until the mixture is a collection of clumps that are approximately the size of sunflower seeds.

2. Add the ice water 2 tablespoons at a time and work the mixture with the pastry cutter until it comes together as a dough. Make sure you work quickly to avoid overworking the dough.

3. Place the dough between two pieces of parchment paper and roll it out to fit the pie plate. Place it in the pie plate, trim any excess, and crimp the edge of the crust. Place the crust in the freezer for 10 minutes.

4. Combine the heavy cream and egg yolk. Remove the crust from the freezer and brush it with the egg wash. Poke holes all over the bottom and sides of the crust, place it in the oven, and bake for 10 minutes.

5. Check the dough to see if it is puffing up. If it is, remove from the oven and poke more holes in the dough. Return to the oven and bake until the crust is just starting to turn golden brown, about 20 minutes. Remove from the oven and let the crust cool.

6. To begin preparations for the filling, place the flour, cocoa powder, salt, and sugar in a mixing bowl and whisk to combine. Set the mixture aside.

7. Place the water and egg yolks in a separate bowl, whisk to combine, and then strain this mixture into the evaporated milk. Add the dry mixture and whisk to combine.

8. Strain the filling into a medium saucepan and bring to a boil over medium heat, stirring constantly.

9. Remove the pan from heat, stir in the vanilla and butter, and beat at medium speed with a handheld mixer fitted with the paddle attachment until smooth. Cover the saucepan and set it aside.

10. Preheat the oven to 325°F. To prepare the meringue, place the egg whites and cream of tartar in the work bowl of a stand mixer fitted with the whisk attachment and beat at high speed until frothy. With the mixer running, gradually incorporate the sugar and beat until the meringue holds stiff peaks.

11. Pour the filling into the crust and top with the meringue, piling it high in the shape of a beehive. Use a spoon to lift the meringue into peaks.

12. Place the pie in the oven and bake until a few cracks form in the meringue, about 45 minutes. Remove from the oven and let cool before serving.

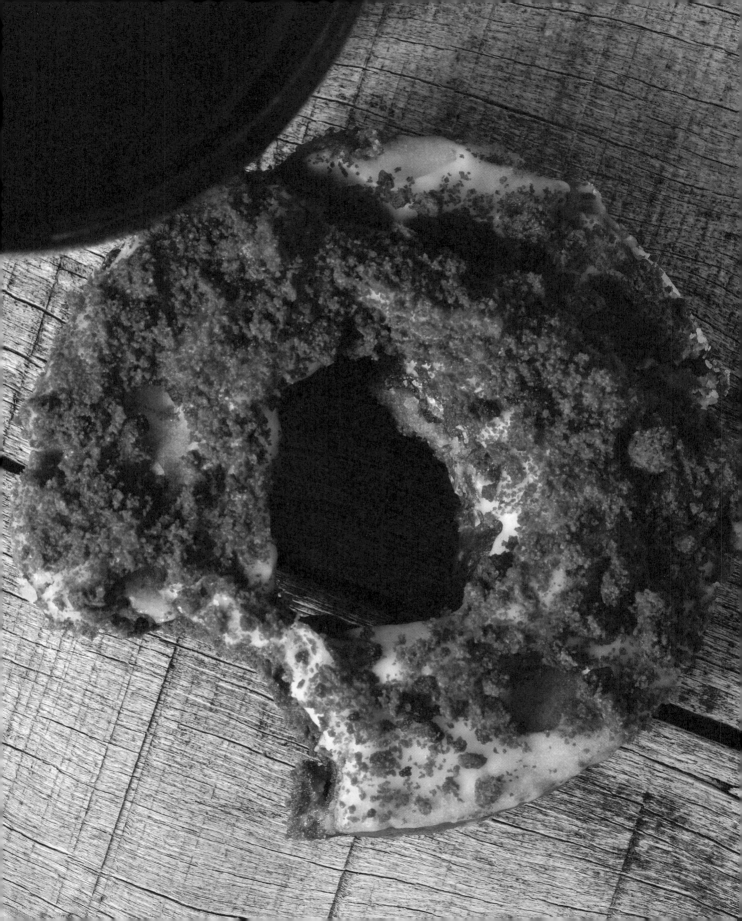

Yield: 12 Doughnuts

Active Time: 1 Hour

Total Time: 24 Hours

INGREDIENTS

6 oz. sugar

1 oz. unsalted butter, softened

3 egg yolks

10.8 oz. sour cream

12.9 oz. all-purpose flour, plus more as needed

1½ oz. cocoa powder

2 teaspoons baking powder

1 tablespoon kosher salt

4 drops of red gel food coloring

Canola oil, as needed

Cream Cheese Frosting (see page 254), for topping

Red icing sugar, for topping

Red Velvet Doughnuts

1. In the work bowl of a stand mixer fitted with the paddle attachment, cream the sugar and butter on medium speed until light and fluffy, about 5 minutes.

2. Incorporate the egg yolks one at a time, scraping down the work bowl as needed. When all of the egg yolks have been incorporated, add the sour cream and beat until incorporated. Add the flour, cocoa powder, baking powder, salt, and food coloring and beat until the mixture comes together as a dough.

3. Coat a medium heatproof bowl with nonstick cooking spray, transfer the dough to the bowl, and cover with plastic wrap. Refrigerate overnight.

4. Add canola oil to a Dutch oven until it is about 2 inches deep and warm it to 350°F. Set a cooling rack in a rimmed baking sheet beside the stove.

5. Remove the dough from the refrigerator and place it on a flour-dusted work surface. Roll the dough out until it is ½ inch thick. Cut out the doughnuts using a round 4-inch cookie cutter and then use a round 1-inch cookie cutter to cut out the centers.

6. Transfer the doughnuts to the wire rack and let them sit at room temperature for 10 minutes.

7. Working in batches, carefully slip the doughnuts into the hot oil and fry, turning them once, until browned and cooked through, about 4 minutes. A cake tester inserted into the sides of the doughnuts should come out clean. Transfer the cooked doughnuts to the wire rack to drain and cool.

8. Spread the frosting over the doughnuts, sprinkle icing sugar over the top, and enjoy.

Yield: 12 Eclairs

Active Time: 40 Minutes

Total Time: 1 Hour and 30 Minutes

INGREDIENTS

17 oz. water

8½ oz. unsalted butter

1 teaspoon fine sea salt

2.4 oz. sugar

12½ oz. all-purpose flour

6 eggs

Pastry Cream (see page 254)

Chocolate Ganache (see page 258), warm

Eclairs

1. Preheat the oven to 425°F and line two baking sheets with parchment paper. In a medium saucepan, combine the water, butter, salt, and sugar and warm the mixture over medium heat until the butter is melted.

2. Add the flour to the pan and use a rubber spatula or wooden spoon to fold the mixture until it comes together as a thick, shiny dough, taking care not to let the dough burn.

3. Transfer the dough to the work bowl of a stand mixer fitted with the paddle attachment and beat on medium speed until the dough is no longer steaming and the bowl is just warm to the touch, at least 10 minutes.

4. Incorporate the eggs two at a time, scraping down the work bowl between each addition. Transfer the dough to a piping bag fit with a plain tip. Pipe 12 eclairs onto the baking sheets, leaving 1½ inches between them. They should be approximately 5 inches long.

5. Place the eclairs in the oven and bake for 10 minutes. Lower the oven's temperature to 325°F and bake until golden brown and a cake tester inserted into their centers comes out clean, 20 to 25 minutes. Remove from the oven and let them cool on a wire rack.

6. Fill a piping bag with the Pastry Cream and fit the piping bag with a plain tip.

7. Using a paring knife, cut 3 small slits on the undersides of the eclairs and fill them with the Pastry Cream.

8. Carefully dip the top halves of the eclairs in the ganache, or drizzle the ganache over the pastries. Allow the chocolate to set before serving.

Yield: 12 Doughnuts

Active Time: 1 Hour

Total Time: 24 Hours

INGREDIENTS

6 oz. sugar

2 tablespoons unsalted butter, softened

3 egg yolks

10.8 oz. sour cream

11.4 oz. all-purpose flour, plus more as needed

2.9 oz. cocoa powder

2 teaspoons baking powder

1 tablespoon kosher salt

Canola oil, as needed

Chocolate Ganache (see page 258), warm

Chocolate Cake Doughnuts

1. In the work bowl of a stand mixer fitted with the paddle attachment, cream the sugar and butter on medium speed until light and fluffy, about 5 minutes.

2. Incorporate the egg yolks one at a time, scraping down the work bowl as needed. When all of the egg yolks have been incorporated, add the sour cream and beat until incorporated. Add the flour, cocoa powder, baking powder, and salt and beat until the mixture comes together as a dough.

3. Coat a medium heatproof bowl with nonstick cooking spray, transfer the dough to the bowl, and cover with plastic wrap. Refrigerate overnight.

4. Add canola oil to a Dutch oven until it is about 2 inches deep and warm it to 350°F. Set a cooling rack in a rimmed baking sheet beside the stove.

5. Remove the dough from the refrigerator and place it on a flour-dusted work surface. Roll the dough out until it is ½ inch thick. Cut out the doughnuts using a round 4-inch cookie cutter and then use a round 1-inch cookie cutter to cut out the centers.

6. Transfer the doughnuts to the wire rack and let them sit at room temperature for 10 minutes.

7. Working in batches, carefully slip the doughnuts into the hot oil and fry, turning them once, until browned and cooked through, about 4 minutes. A cake tester inserted into the sides of the doughnuts should come out clean. Transfer the cooked doughnuts to the wire rack to drain and cool.

8. When cool, dip the top half of the doughnuts in the ganache, place them on a piece of parchment paper, and let the chocolate set before enjoying.

INGREDIENTS

½ cup whole milk

32 large marshmallows

¼ cup green crème de menthe

¼ cup white crème de cacao

1½ cups Whipped Cream (see page 255)

2 drops of green gel food coloring

1 oreo crust (see page 118)

Grasshopper Pie

1. Place the milk and marshmallows in a large saucepan and cook over low heat, stirring frequently, until the marshmallows have melted. Place the pan in the refrigerator and chill for 20 minutes, stirring occasionally.

2. Stir the crème de menthe and crème de cacao into the mixture. Fold the marshmallow mixture into the Whipped Cream and then stir in the green food coloring.

3. Place the filling in the crust and smooth the top with a rubber spatula. Place in the refrigerator and chill for 4 hours before serving.

Yield: 6 Pastries

Active Time: 50 Minutes

Total Time: 2 Hours

INGREDIENTS

17 oz. water

8½ oz. unsalted butter

1 teaspoon fine sea salt

2.4 oz. sugar

12½ oz. all-purpose flour

7 eggs

1 cup slivered almonds

Hazelnut Mousseline (see page 256)

Confectioners' sugar, for dusting

Paris-Brest

1. Preheat the oven to 425°F and line two baking sheets with parchment paper. In a medium saucepan, combine the water, butter, salt, and sugar and warm the mixture over medium heat until the butter is melted.

2. Add the flour to the pan and use a rubber spatula or wooden spoon to fold the mixture until it comes together as a thick, shiny dough, taking care not to let the dough burn.

3. Transfer the dough to the work bowl of a stand mixer fitted with the paddle attachment and beat on medium speed until the dough is no longer steaming and the bowl is just warm to the touch, at least 10 minutes.

4. Incorporate six of the eggs two at a time, scraping down the work bowl between each addition. Transfer the dough to a piping bag and fit the piping bag with an 867 tip (this will be called a "French Star Tip" on occasion).

5. Pipe a 5-inch ring of dough onto a baking sheet and then pipe another ring inside the first ring. Pipe another ring atop the seam between the first two rings. Repeat until all of the dough has been used.

6. In a small bowl, whisk the remaining egg and brush the tops of the dough with it. Arrange the almonds on top and gently press down to ensure they adhere.

7. Place the pastries in the oven and bake for 10 minutes. Lower the oven's temperature to 300°F and bake until golden brown and a cake tester inserted into each one comes out clean, 30 to 35 minutes. Remove from the oven and let them cool on a wire rack.

8. Place the mousseline in a piping bag and fit the piping bag with a plain tip. Using a serrated knife, slice the pastries in half along their equators. Pipe rosettes of the mousseline around the inside. Place the top half of the pastries on top, dust them with confectioners' sugar, and enjoy.

Paris-Brest
see page 157

Yield: 10 Cannoli

Active Time: 45 Minutes

Total Time: 4 Hours

INGREDIENTS

¾ lb. whole-milk ricotta cheese

¾ lb. mascarpone cheese

4 oz. chocolate, grated

¾ cup confectioners' sugar, plus more for dusting

1½ teaspoons pure vanilla extract

Pinch of fine sea salt

10 cannoli shells

Cannoli

1. Line a colander with three pieces of cheesecloth and place it in the sink. Place the ricotta in the colander, form the cheesecloth into a pouch, and twist to remove as much liquid as possible from the ricotta. Keep the pouch taut and twisted, place it in a baking dish, and place a cast-iron skillet on top. Weigh the skillet down with two large, heavy cans and place in the refrigerator for 1 hour.

2. Discard the drained liquid and transfer the ricotta to a mixing bowl. Add the mascarpone, half of the grated chocolate, the confectioners' sugar, vanilla, and salt and stir until well combined. Cover the bowl and refrigerate for at least 1 hour. The mixture will keep in the refrigerator for up to 24 hours.

3. Line an 18 x 13–inch baking sheet with parchment paper. Fill a small saucepan halfway with water and bring it to a gentle simmer. Place the remaining chocolate in a heatproof mixing bowl, place it over the simmering water, and stir until it is melted.

4. Dip the ends of the cannoli shells in the melted chocolate, let the excess drip off, and transfer them to the baking sheet. Let the shells sit until the chocolate is firm, about 1 hour.

5. Place the cannoli filling in a piping bag and cut a ½-inch slit in it. Pipe the filling into the shells, working from both ends to ensure they are filled evenly. When all of the cannoli have been filled, dust them with confectioners' sugar and enjoy.

Yield: 16 Croissants

Active Time: 30 Minutes

Total Time: 2 Hours

INGREDIENTS

Croissant Dough (see pages 262-263)

All-purpose flour, as needed

2 cups dark chocolate coins (55 percent), chopped

1 egg, beaten

Confectioners' sugar, for dusting

Pain au Chocolat

1. Line two baking sheets with parchment paper.

2. Place the dough on a flour-dusted work surface and roll it into an 8 x 20–inch rectangle. Using a pizza cutter or chef's knife, cut the dough horizontally in the center so that you have two 4 x 20–inch rectangles. Cut each rectangle vertically into strips that are 5 inches wide.

3. Cut each rectangle in half at its equator, yielding 16 rectangles. Gently roll out each rectangle until it is 8 inches long.

4. Place 2 tablespoons of chocolate on one end of each rectangle and roll the rectangles up tightly.

5. Place eight croissants on each of the baking sheets. Cover the baking sheets with plastic wrap and let the croissants rest at room temperature for 1 hour.

6. Preheat the oven to 375ºF.

7. Remove the plastic wrap and brush the croissants with the beaten egg.

8. Place the croissants in the oven and bake until they are golden brown, 20 to 22 minutes.

9. Remove the croissants from the oven and place them on wire racks. Let the croissants cool slightly before dusting them with confectioners' sugar and enjoying.

PUDDINGS, CUSTARDS & ICE CREAM

These desserts are humble in their construction, yes. But so delicious and comforting that they carry an ability all too rare in this world: making you realize how little one needs to actually be happy. Many of the preparations in this chapter are easily available at the store. And while those items can certainly scratch the itch when you need some chocolate, these recipes are here to remind you that convenience always comes at a cost.

INGREDIENTS

For the Trifle

4 tablespoons unsalted butter, melted, plus more as needed

3 eggs

⅔ cup sugar

¼ cup sour cream

½ teaspoon orange zest

¼ cup cherry liqueur

⅔ cup cake flour

⅓ cup all-purpose flour

½ cup cocoa powder

1 teaspoon baking powder

¼ teaspoon baking soda

1½ teaspoons fine sea salt

2 cups Roasted Vanilla Cherries (see page 259), quartered

¼ cup water, at room temperature

For the Cocoa Crumble

1 cup confectioners' sugar

⅔ cup all-purpose flour

½ cup unsweetened cocoa powder

½ cup unsalted butter, melted

Whipped Cream (see page 255)

Black Forest Trifle

1. Preheat the oven to 350°F and coat a round 9-inch cake pan with butter. To begin preparations for the trifle, place the eggs and sugar in the work bowl of a stand mixer fitted with the paddle attachment and beat until pale and fluffy. Add the butter, sour cream, orange zest, and half of the cherry liqueur and beat until combined.

2. Sift the flours, cocoa powder, baking powder, baking soda, and salt into a separate mixing bowl. Add the mixture to the work bowl of the stand mixer and beat until the mixture comes together as a smooth batter.

3. Pour the batter into the cake pan, place it in the oven, and bake until a cake tester inserted into the center of the cake comes out clean, 20 to 25 minutes. Remove the cake from the oven and let it cool in the pan for 10 minutes before removing it from the pan and placing it on a wire rack to cool completely. Keep the oven on.

4. Place the cherries and the remaining liqueur in a bowl and let the mixture sit for at least 30 minutes. Strain, set the cherries aside, and combine the strained liquid with the water. Set the mixture aside.

5. Line a baking sheet with parchment paper. To prepare the crumble, sift the sugar, flour, and cocoa powder into a mixing bowl. Add the melted butter and work the mixture with a fork until it is crumbly. Place the mixture on the parchment-lined baking sheet in an even layer, place it in the oven, and bake until it is crispy, about 25 minutes. Remove the pan from the oven and let the crumble cool completely.

6. When you are ready to assemble the trifle, cut the cake into 1½-inch cubes. Cover the bottom of a 3-quart trifle bowl with some of the cake, breaking pieces as needed to fill up any empty space. Brush the pieces of cake with the reserved liqueur-and-water mixture. Top with layers of Whipped Cream, cherries, and crumble and then repeat this layering process two more times. Top the trifle with a layer of Whipped Cream, sprinkle any remaining cherries and crumble over it, and enjoy.

Yield: 6 Servings

Active Time: 30 Minutes

Total Time: 2 Hours and 45 Minutes

INGREDIENTS

10½ oz. white chocolate

14 oz. heavy cream

2 oz. molasses

1 oz. confectioners' sugar

2 egg yolks

2 eggs

1 teaspoon pure vanilla extract

1 teaspoon cinnamon

1 teaspoon allspice

1 teaspoon cardamom

1 teaspoon freshly grated nutmeg

½ teaspoon ground ginger

2 cups Whipped Cream (see page 255), for topping

White Chocolate & Gingerbread Mousse

1. Fill a small saucepan halfway with water and bring it to a simmer. Place the white chocolate in a heatproof mixing bowl and place it over the simmering water. Stir until the chocolate is melted and smooth, remove it from heat, and set it aside.

2. In the work bowl of a stand mixer fitted with the whisk attachment, whip the heavy cream until it holds soft peaks. Transfer the whipped cream to another bowl and place it in the refrigerator.

3. Wipe out the work bowl of the stand mixer, add the molasses, confectioners' sugar, egg yolks, eggs, vanilla, cinnamon, allspice, cardamom, nutmeg, and ginger and whip until the mixture has doubled in size and is pale, about 15 minutes. Transfer the mixture to a mixing bowl. Add the melted chocolate and whisk to incorporate. Add the whipped cream and fold to incorporate it.

4. Divide the mousse among six 8-oz. ramekins and lightly tap the bottom of each one on the counter to settle the mousse and remove any air bubbles. Transfer the mousse to the refrigerator and chill for 2 hours.

5. To serve, top each mousse with Whipped Cream and enjoy.

Yield: 6 Servings

Active Time: 15 Minutes

Total Time: 3 Hours

INGREDIENTS

¼ cup stevia or preferred keto-friendly sweetener

1¼ oz. Baker's Chocolate, grated

¼ cup unsweetened cocoa powder

¼ cup almond flour

½ teaspoon kosher salt

2 cups whole milk

¼ cup heavy cream

4 tablespoons unsalted butter, divided into tablespoons

2 teaspoons pure vanilla extract

Keto Chocolate Pudding

1. Place the sweetener, chocolate, cocoa powder, almond flour, and salt in a saucepan and whisk to combine. Cook over medium heat and slowly add the milk, whisking continually. Cook until the mixture thickens and comes to a boil, approximately 8 to 10 minutes.

2. Reduce the heat to low and simmer the mixture for 1 to 2 minutes. Remove the saucepan from heat and stir in the cream.

3. Incorporate the butter 1 tablespoon at a time and then stir in the vanilla.

4. Transfer the pudding into the serving dishes and place plastic wrap directly on the surface to prevent a skin from forming. Refrigerate the pudding for 2 hours before serving.

Nutritional Info Per Serving: Calories: 153; Fat: 12 g; Net Carbs: 7 g; Protein: 5.2 g

Yield: 6 Servings

Active Time: 30 Minutes

Total Time: 6 Hours and 30 Minutes

INGREDIENTS

5 oz. chocolate

2 cups heavy cream

4 oz. sugar

4 egg yolks

1 tablespoon chocolate liqueur

¼ teaspoon kosher salt

Chocolate Pots de Crème

1. Preheat the oven to 325°F. Bring 8 cups of water to a boil and then set aside.

2. Place the chocolate in a heatproof mixing bowl. Place the heavy cream in a saucepan and bring it to a simmer over medium heat. Pour the cream over the chocolate and whisk until the chocolate has melted and the mixture is combined. Set the mixture aside.

3. In the work bowl of a stand mixer fitted with the whisk attachment, combine the sugar, egg yolks, liqueur, and salt and whip on high until the mixture is pale yellow and ribbony, about 10 minutes.

4. Pour the mixture into the chocolate mixture and fold to incorporate.

5. Fill six 8-oz. ramekins three-quarters of the way with the custard.

6. Place the ramekins in a 13 x 9–inch baking pan and pour the boiling water into the pan until it reaches halfway up the sides of the ramekins. Place the pan in the oven and bake until the custards are set at their edges and jiggle slightly at their centers, about 50 minutes. Remove the custards from the oven and carefully transfer the ramekins to a wire rack. Let them cool for 1 hour.

7. Place the ramekins in the refrigerator and chill them for 4 hours before enjoying.

Yield: 3 Cups

Active Time: 15 Minutes

Total Time: 15 Minutes

INGREDIENTS

1½ cups heavy cream

½ lb. chocolate

½ cup water

2 tablespoons cocoa powder

1 tablespoon confectioners' sugar

1 teaspoon pure vanilla extract

Pinch of kosher salt

Quick Chocolate Mousse

1. Place the heavy cream in the work bowl of a stand mixer fitted with the whisk attachment and whip it on medium until the cream holds stiff peaks.

2. Fill a small saucepan halfway with water and bring it to a gentle simmer.

3. Combine the chocolate, water, cocoa powder, confectioners' sugar, vanilla, and salt in a heatproof mixing bowl. Place the bowl over the simmering water and whisk until the chocolate has melted and the mixture is smooth.

4. Remove the bowl from heat, add the whipped cream, and fold until incorporated. Transfer the mousse to ramekins or a piping bag, if using it as a cake filling. If not using immediately, place the mousse in an airtight container and store it in the refrigerator, where it will keep for up to 2 weeks.

17 oz. dark chocolate (55 to 65 percent)

19 oz. heavy cream

2 egg yolks

1 oz. sugar

½ cup whole milk

¼ teaspoon kosher salt

Whipped Cream (see page 255), for serving

Dark Chocolate Mousse

1. Fill a small saucepan halfway with water and bring it to a simmer. Place the dark chocolate in a heatproof mixing bowl and place it over the simmering water. Stir until the chocolate is melted and then set aside.

2. In the work bowl of a stand mixer fitted with the whisk attachment, whip 15 oz. of the heavy cream until it holds soft peaks. Transfer the whipped cream to another bowl and place it in the refrigerator.

3. Place the egg yolks and sugar in a mixing bowl, whisk to combine, and set the mixture aside.

4. In a small saucepan, combine the milk, salt, and remaining cream and bring the mixture to a simmer. Remove the pan from heat.

5. Whisking constantly, gradually add the warm mixture to the egg yolk mixture. When all of the warm mixture has been incorporated, add the tempered egg yolks to the saucepan and cook over low heat, stirring constantly, until the mixture thickens enough to coat the back of a wooden spoon.

6. Remove the pan from heat, pour the mixture into the melted chocolate, and whisk until thoroughly combined. Add half of the whipped cream, fold until incorporated, and then fold in the rest of the whipped cream.

7. Divide the mousse among six 8-oz. ramekins and lightly tap the bottom of each one on the counter to settle the mousse and remove any air bubbles. Transfer the mousse to the refrigerator and chill for 2 hours.

8. To serve, top each mousse with Whipped Cream and enjoy.

Yield: 8 Servings

Active Time: 15 Minutes

Total Time: 2 Hours and 15 Minutes

INGREDIENTS

3 large egg yolks

¼ cup sugar

½ cup cocoa powder

2 tablespoons cornstarch

¾ teaspoon fine sea salt

2½ cups whole milk

6 tablespoons unsalted butter, softened

2 teaspoons pure vanilla extract

Shredded coconut, for topping (optional)

Raspberries, for topping (optional)

Milk chocolate, grated, for topping (optional)

Chocolate Pudding

1. Place the egg yolks in a heatproof bowl and whisk to combine.

2. Place the sugar, cocoa powder, cornstarch, and salt in a saucepan and whisk to combine. Cook over medium heat and, whisking continually, gradually add the milk. Cook until the mixture thickens and comes to a simmer, approximately 8 to 10 minutes.

3. Reduce the heat to low and simmer for 1 to 2 minutes. Remove the saucepan from heat and stir in the butter and vanilla.

4. While whisking continually, gradually add the warm milk mixture to the egg yolks. When all of the milk mixture has been incorporated, transfer the pudding into serving dishes and place plastic wrap directly on the pudding's surface to prevent a skin from forming. Place in the refrigerator and chill for 2 hours before topping as desired and serving.

Yield: 16 Servings

Active Time: 45 Minutes

Total Time: 24 Hours

INGREDIENTS

8 cups sourdough bread pieces

2 cups chocolate chips

3 cups whole milk

3 tablespoons unsalted butter

2¼ cups sugar

¾ cup heavy cream

1½ teaspoons cinnamon

½ teaspoon freshly grated nutmeg

¼ teaspoon kosher salt

3 eggs

1½ teaspoons pure vanilla extract

Chocolate & Sourdough Bread Pudding

1. Place the bread in a mixing bowl and let it rest overnight at room temperature, uncovered, to dry out.

2. Place the chocolate chips in a heatproof mixing bowl. Place the milk, butter, sugar, cream, cinnamon, nutmeg, and salt in a medium saucepan and bring the mixture to a simmer. Remove the pan from heat, pour it over the chocolate chips, and stir until the chocolate has melted and the mixture is combined.

3. Place the eggs and vanilla in a heatproof mixing bowl and whisk to combine. Whisking constantly, gradually add the melted chocolate mixture until all of it has been incorporated.

4. Coat a 13 x 9–inch baking pan with cooking spray and then distribute the bread pieces in it. Slowly pour the custard over the bread and gently shake the pan to ensure it is evenly distributed. Press down on the bread with a rubber spatula so that it soaks up the custard. Cover the baking pan with aluminum foil, place it in the refrigerator, and chill for 2 hours.

5. Preheat the oven to 350°F.

6. Place the baking pan in the oven and bake for 45 minutes. Remove the aluminum foil and bake until the bread pudding is golden brown on top, about 15 minutes. Remove from the oven and let the bread pudding cool slightly before slicing and serving.

INGREDIENTS

3 cups heavy cream

1 cup whole milk

½ cup sugar

½ cup light corn syrup or ⅓ cup honey

½ teaspoon fine sea salt

Philadelphia Ice Cream Base

1. In a saucepan, combine the cream, milk, sugar, corn syrup or honey, and salt and bring the mixture to a simmer, stirring until the sugar has dissolved.

2. Pour the mixture into a heatproof bowl and let it cool to room temperature. Cover it with plastic wrap and store in the refrigerator for at least 4 hours.

3. Flavor the ice cream base as desired and churn it in an ice cream maker until it has the desired consistency.

Yield: 1 Quart

Active Time: 30 Minutes

Total Time: 5 Hours

INGREDIENTS

2 cups heavy cream

1 cup whole milk

⅔ cup sugar

⅛ teaspoon fine sea salt

6 large egg yolks

Custard Ice Cream Base

1. In a small saucepan, combine the heavy cream, milk, sugar, and salt and bring to a simmer over medium-low heat, stirring until the sugar completely dissolves, about 5 minutes.

2. Remove the saucepan from heat. Place the egg yolks in a heat-proof mixing bowl and whisk them until combined. While whisking constantly, slowly whisk about a third of the hot cream mixture into the yolks. Whisk the tempered egg yolks into the saucepan.

3. Warm the mixture over medium-low heat, stirring constantly, until the mixture is thick enough to coat the back of a wooden spoon (about 170°F on an instant-read thermometer).

4. Strain the custard through a fine-mesh sieve into a bowl and let it cool to room temperature. Cover the bowl, place it in the refrigerator, and let it chill for at least 4 hours.

5. Flavor the custard as desired and churn it in an ice cream maker until it has the desired consistency.

Custard Ice Cream Base

see page 183

Yield: 1 Quart

Active Time: 30 Minutes

Total Time: 9 Hours

INGREDIENTS

1 quart ice cream base

¾ cup heavy cream

3 tablespoons cocoa powder

4 oz. chocolate, chopped

¾ cup crème fraîche

1 teaspoon pure vanilla extract

Chocolate Ice Cream

1. While the ice cream base is still warm, combine the cream and cocoa powder in a saucepan and bring to a simmer over medium-low heat.

2. Place the chocolate in a heatproof bowl and pour the warm cream mixture over it. Stir until melted and smooth.

3. Stir the melted chocolate mixture, crème fraîche, and vanilla into the base. Let the mixture cool to room temperature. Strain into a bowl through a fine-mesh sieve, cover the bowl, and store in the refrigerator for 4 hours.

4. Churn the mixture in an ice cream maker until it reaches the desired consistency. Place the ice cream in an airtight container and freeze it for 4 to 6 hours before serving.

Yield: 6 Servings

Active Time: 10 Minutes

Total Time: 8 Hours

INGREDIENTS

1½ cups heavy cream

¾ cup whole milk

¼ cup unsweetened cocoa powder

½ cup stevia or preferred keto-friendly sweetener

3 large egg yolks, lightly beaten

1¾ oz. Baker's Chocolate, chopped

½ teaspoon pure vanilla extract

Pinch of flaky sea salt

1½ tablespoons vodka (optional)

Keto Chocolate Ice Cream

1. Prepare an ice bath in a large bowl. Place the cream, ½ cup of the milk, the cocoa powder, and sweetener in a saucepan and warm the mixture over medium heat, stirring continually. Once the sugar has dissolved, take approximately 1 cup from the mixture in the saucepan and whisk it into the bowl containing the egg yolks. Add the tempered egg yolks to the saucepan and continue cooking over medium heat, stirring continually, until the custard has thickened to where it will coat the back of a wooden spoon. Remove the pan from heat.

2. Stir the chocolate into the custard, let the mixture cool for 5 minutes, and then stir until it is smooth. Pour the custard into a metal bowl and then set the bowl in the ice bath. Stir occasionally until the mixture is smooth, about 10 minutes. Cover the bowl with plastic wrap and refrigerate for 3 hours.

3. Stir the remaining milk, the vanilla, salt, and vodka (if using) into the chilled custard. Pour the custard into an ice cream maker and churn until the ice cream has the desired consistency, about 20 minutes. Pour the ice cream into an airtight container, cover, and freeze until firm, about 4 hours.

Tip: Using the vodka will help prevent the formation of ice crystals in the ice cream without affecting the flavor, ultimately yielding a smoother texture.

Nutritional Info Per Serving: Calories: 311; Fat: 29.6 g; Net Carbs: 6.8 g; Protein: 5.2 g

Chocolate Ice Cream

see page 186

Yield: 1 Quart

Active Time: 30 Minutes

Total Time: 9 Hours

INGREDIENTS

1 cup fresh mint leaves

½ cup sugar

1 quart ice cream base
(no sugar)

1 cup chopped dark chocolate

Mint Chocolate Chip Ice Cream

1. Place the mint leaves and sugar in a food processor and pulse until well combined.

2. Prepare the base, adding the mint-and-sugar mixture in place of the plain sugar in your chosen preparation. When the base is ready, pour the mixture into a heatproof bowl and let it steep for 30 minutes.

3. Strain into a bowl through a fine-mesh sieve, cover the bowl, and refrigerate for 4 hours.

4. Churn the base in an ice cream maker until it is almost the desired consistency. Add the chocolate and churn until evenly distributed. Place the ice cream in an airtight container and freeze it for 4 to 6 hours before serving.

Yield: 4 Servings

Active Time: 5 Minutes

Total Time: 5 Minutes

INGREDIENTS

Hot Fudge (see page 258)

2 pints of vanilla ice cream

Whipped Cream
(see page 255)

½ cup chopped pecans
or walnuts, for topping

4 maraschino cherries,
for topping

Hot Fudge Sundaes

1. Place the Hot Fudge in the bottom of four tulip sundae dishes or bowls.

2. Scoop the ice cream into the bowls.

3. Top each portion with Whipped Cream, pecans or walnuts, and a maraschino cherry and serve.

Yield: 4 Servings

Active Time: 10 Minutes

Total Time: 1 Hour and
45 Minutes

INGREDIENTS

**Dough from Chocolate Chip
Cookies (see page 13)**

1 pint of ice cream

Classic Ice Cream Sandwiches

1. Preheat the oven to 350°F and line two baking sheets with parchment paper.

2. Drop 4-oz. portions of the dough on the baking sheets, making sure to leave enough space between them. Place them in the oven and bake until golden brown and the edges are set, 14 to 18 minutes.

3. Remove the cookies from the oven and transfer them to wire racks to cool completely.

4. When the cookies have cooled completely, scoop ice cream onto half of the cookies. Carefully press down with the other cookies to assemble the sandwiches and store in the freezer until ready to serve.

BEVERAGES

After a particularly great meal, one does not always have enough space remaining to enjoy the richness of a cake, brownie, or pastry. But the chocolate lover still needs something to provide a fitting end to the day, a small treat that will soothe and leaven the mind as it muses on all that has passed today and what will come tomorrow. These recipes are made for such moments, providing the flavor that you crave, in a far more consumable package.

Yield: 1 Drink

Active Time: 2 Minutes

Total Time: 2 Minutes

INGREDIENTS

1¾ oz. blended Scotch whisky

2 teaspoons Amontillado sherry

1½ teaspoons pear liqueur

1 teaspoon white crème de cacao

1 teaspoon Cointreau

½ teaspoon Simple Syrup (see page 260)

2 dashes of Angostura bitters

lemon twist, for garnish

Mind Maps

1. Chill a coupe in the freezer.

2. Place all of the ingredients in the chilled coupe and stir to combine.

3. Garnish with the lemon twist and enjoy.

Yield: 1 Drink

Active Time: 2 Minutes

Total Time: 10 Minutes

INGREDIENTS

3 oz. freshly brewed coffee

1 teaspoon honey

2 oz. heavy cream, chilled

1 oz. vodka

1 teaspoon Chocolate Ganache (see page 258)

3 chocolate-covered espresso beans, for garnish

Moment to Moment

1. While the espresso or coffee is still hot, stir the honey into it. Chill the mixture in the refrigerator.

2. Place the sweetened espresso or coffee, heavy cream, vodka, and ganache in a cocktail shaker and shake vigorously until chilled.

3. Double strain into a cocktail glass, garnish with the chocolate-covered espresso beans, and enjoy.

Yield: 1 Drink

Active Time: 2 Minutes

Total Time: 2 Minutes

INGREDIENTS

1½ oz. aged rum

¾ oz. fresh lime juice

½ oz. crème de cacao

½ oz. Simple Syrup
(see page 260)

Eyes of My Mind

1. Chill a cocktail glass in the freezer.

2. Place all of the ingredients in a cocktail shaker, fill it two-thirds of the way with ice, and shake vigorously until chilled.

3. Strain into the chilled cocktail glass and enjoy.

Yield: 1 Drink

Active Time: 2 Minutes

Total Time: 2 Minutes

INGREDIENTS

1½ oz. vodka

1½ oz. Kahlúa

1½ oz. Baileys Irish Cream

**¾ cup chocolate ice cream
(see page 186 for homemade)**

½ cup ice

**Whipped Cream (see page
255), for garnish**

Chocolate chips, for garnish

Mudslide

1. Place the vodka, liqueurs, ice cream, and ice in a blender and puree to the desired consistency.

2. Pour the cocktail into a tumbler, garnish with Whipped Cream and chocolate chips, and enjoy.

Yield: 4 Servings

Active Time: 2 Minutes

Total Time: 2 Minutes

INGREDIENTS

2 pints of chocolate ice cream (see page 186 for homemade)

½ cup whole milk

½ teaspoon fine sea salt

2 teaspoons pure vanilla extract

Whipped Cream (see page 255), for garnish

Chocolate, grated, for garnish

Chocolate Milkshakes

1. Place all of the ingredients, except for the garnishes, in a blender and puree until combined.

2. Pour the milkshakes into tall glasses, garnish each one with Whipped Cream and chocolate, and enjoy.

Yield: 4 Servings

Active Time: 15 Minutes

Total Time: 15 Minutes

INGREDIENTS

3 cups whole milk

1 cup half-and-half

3 cinnamon sticks

1 red chile pepper, stem and seeds removed

¼ cup sweetened condensed milk

1½ lbs. semisweet chocolate chips

½ teaspoon pure vanilla extract

1 teaspoon freshly grated nutmeg

½ teaspoon fine sea salt

Whipped Cream (see page 255), for topping

Mexican Hot Chocolate

1. Place the milk, half-and-half, cinnamon sticks, and chile in a saucepan and warm it over medium-low heat for 5 to 6 minutes, making sure the mixture does not come to a boil. When the mixture starts to steam, remove the cinnamon sticks and chile pepper and discard them.

2. Add the sweetened condensed milk and whisk until combined. Add the chocolate chips and cook, stirring occasionally, until they have melted. Stir in the vanilla, nutmeg, and salt.

3. Ladle the hot chocolate into warmed mugs, top with Whipped Cream, and enjoy.

Yield: 10 Servings

Active Time: 10 Minutes

Total Time: 20 Minutes

INGREDIENTS

8 cups whole milk

1 cup heavy cream

½ cup sugar, plus more to taste

½ cup freshly brewed espresso

½ lb. bittersweet chocolate, chopped

1 tablespoon orange zest

½ teaspoon fine sea salt

Whipped Cream (see page 255), for topping

Café Mocha

1. Place the milk, cream, sugar, and espresso in a saucepan and warm it over medium heat.

2. Place the chocolate in a heatproof bowl. When the milk mixture is hot, ladle 1 cup of it over the chocolate and whisk until the chocolate is completely melted, adding more of the warm milk mixture if the melted chocolate mixture is too thick.

3. Pour the melted chocolate mixture into the pot of warm milk and whisk to combine. Add the orange zest and salt and stir to combine.

4. Pour the beverage into mugs, top with Whipped Cream, and enjoy.

Yield: 1 Drink

Active Time: 2 Minutes

Total Time: 2 Minutes

INGREDIENTS

1 oz. FEW Bourbon

¾ oz. Kahlúa

2 teaspoons Orgeat
(see page 259)

¾ oz. Frangelico

¾ oz. Mozart Dark Chocolate
liqueur

1 tablespoon peanut butter

1½ oz. whole milk

1 miniature Snickers bar

Marathon Man

1. Add all of the ingredients to a blender along with two large ice cubes and pulverize until there are fine bubbles throughout and all of the ice has been thoroughly incorporated.

2. Pour over ice into a rocks glass and enjoy.

Yield: 1 Drink

Active Time: 2 Minutes

Total Time: 2 Minutes

INGREDIENTS

2 oz. Pinnacle Cake Vodka

1 oz. Marie Brizard Chocolat Royal liqueur

Baileys Irish Cream, to top

Cake crumbs, for garnish

Cake Boss

1. Place a cocktail glass in the freezer.

2. Add the vodka and chocolate liqueur to a cocktail shaker, fill it two-thirds of the way with ice, and shake vigorously until chilled.

3. Strain the cocktail into the chilled cocktail glass.

4. Pour the Baileys over the back of an upturned spoon to float it on top of the cocktail. Garnish with the cake crumbs and enjoy.

Yield: 1 Drink

Active Time: 2 Minutes

Total Time: 2 Minutes

INGREDIENTS

Graham cracker crumbs, for the rim

Chocolate shavings, for the rim

1½ oz. bourbon

1½ oz. Giffard Crème de Cacao (white)

12 oz. chocolate stout, to top

1 toasted marshmallow, for garnish

Campfire S'Mores

1. Place the graham cracker crumbs and chocolate shavings in a dish and stir to combine. Wet the rim of a pint glass and dip it into the mixture.

2. Add the bourbon and crème de cacao to a cocktail shaker, fill it two-thirds of the way with ice, shake vigorously until chilled, and strain into the rimmed pint glass.

3. Top the cocktail with the stout, garnish with the toasted marshmallow, and enjoy.

Yield: 1 Drink

Active Time: 2 Minutes

Total Time: 2 Minutes

INGREDIENTS

2 oz. Burdock & Cacao Nib Brandy (see page 260)

½ oz. chocolate liqueur

2 bar spoons of Pedro Ximénez sherry

1 bar spoon of real maple syrup

3 dashes of orange bitters

Chocolate Burdock Martini

1. Add all of the ingredients to a cocktail shaker, fill it two-thirds of the way with ice, and shake vigorously until chilled.

2. Strain the cocktail into a coupe containing 1 large block of ice and enjoy.

Yield: 1 Drink

Active Time: 2 Minutes

Total Time: 2 Minutes

INGREDIENTS

1½ oz. brandy or Cognac

1 oz. crème de cacao

¾ oz. heavy cream

Brandy Alexander

1. Chill a cocktail glass in the freezer.

2. Place the ingredients in a cocktail shaker, fill it two-thirds of the way with ice, and shake vigorously until chilled.

3. Strain the cocktail into the chilled cocktail glass and enoy.

Yield: 1 Drink

Active Time: 2 Minutes

Total Time: 2 Minutes

INGREDIENTS

1 oz. vodka

1 oz. chocolate liqueur

1 oz. Kahlúa

2 oz. milk

My Silks and Fine Array

1. Add all of the ingredients to a cocktail shaker, fill it two-thirds of the way with ice, and shake vigorously until chilled.

2. Strain the cocktail over ice into a rocks glass and enjoy.

Yield: 1 Drink

Active Time: 2 Minutes

Total Time: 2 Minutes

INGREDIENTS

1 oz. green crème de menthe

1 oz. white crème de cacao

1 oz. heavy cream

Grasshopper

1. Chill a cocktail glass in the freezer.

2. Place all of the ingredients in a cocktail shaker, fill it two-thirds of the way with ice, and shake until chilled.

3. Strain the cocktail into the chilled cocktail glass and enjoy.

CANDIES & OTHER DECADENT TREATS

This last section is for the chocolate purist, those who work a trip to the local chocolatier or sweet shop into their daily walk, who can't resist the selection of treats waiting by the register at the grocery store. From the luscious simplicity of a truffle to the absolute perfection of the peanut butter cup, this chapter tweaks your one true love only slightly, but always for the better.

Yield: 6 to 8 Servings

Active Time: 10 Minutes

Total Time: 40 Minutes

INGREDIENTS

1 lb. white chocolate, chopped

½ cup dried cherries or cranberries

½ cup chopped pistachios

White Chocolate Bark

1. Bring a few inches of water to a simmer in a medium saucepan. Place the chocolate in a heatproof bowl, place it over the simmering water, and stir until it is melted and smooth.

2. Line a rimmed baking sheet with parchment paper. Pour the melted chocolate onto the baking sheet and spread it into an even layer.

3. Sprinkle the cherries and pistachios onto the chocolate and lightly press down on them to ensure that they adhere. Place the baking sheet in the refrigerator and chill until set, about 30 minutes.

4. When the chocolate has set, break the bark up into large pieces and serve.

Yield: 8 Servings

Active Time: 10 Minutes

Total Time: 2 Hours and 10 Minutes

INGREDIENTS

2 pints of fresh strawberries

2 cups semisweet chocolate chips

Chocolate-Dipped Strawberries

1. Line a baking sheet with parchment paper. Rinse the strawberries well and pat them dry.

2. Fill a small saucepan halfway with water and bring it to a simmer. Place the chocolate chips in a heatproof bowl, place it over the simmering water, and stir occasionally until the chocolate has melted.

3. Dip each strawberry into the chocolate halfway, or completely, whichever you prefer.

4. Place the strawberries on the baking sheet, place it in the refrigerator, and chill for at least 2 hours before serving.

Yield: 24 Cookies

Active Time: 15 Minutes

Total Time: 3 Hours

INGREDIENTS

½ lb. unsalted butter, softened

2 lbs. confectioners' sugar

½ cup bourbon

½ teaspoon fine sea salt

Melted chocolate or cocoa powder, for topping

Bourbon Balls

1. Place the butter and half of the confectioners' sugar in the work bowl of a stand mixer fitted with the paddle attachment and beat at low speed to combine. Increase the speed to high and beat until the mixture is light and fluffy. Add the remaining confectioners' sugar, the bourbon, and salt and beat for 2 minutes. Transfer the mixture to the refrigerator and chill until firm, about 2 hours.

2. Line baking sheets with parchment paper and form tablespoons of the butter-and-bourbon mixture into balls. Coat the balls in melted chocolate or cocoa powder and then transfer the baking sheets to the refrigerator. Chill for 45 minutes before serving.

Yield: 24 Balls

Active Time: 20 Minutes

Total Time: 1 Hour

INGREDIENTS

2 tablespoons espresso powder

2 tablespoons boiling water

4 oz. unsalted butter, cut into small pieces and softened

2.3 oz. sugar

1 large egg, at room temperature

½ teaspoon pure vanilla extract

3¾ oz. unsweetened cocoa powder

6.7 oz. all-purpose flour

Pinch of fine sea salt

Mocha Balls

1. Preheat the oven to 350°F.

2. Place the espresso powder and water in a small bowl and stir until the powder has dissolved. Set aside and let cool.

3. Place the butter and sugar in the work bowl of a stand mixer fitted with the paddle attachment and beat at medium speed until light and fluffy. Add the egg and vanilla, beat until well combined, and then add ¾ oz. of the cocoa powder and the espresso mixture. Beat until combined, scraping down the bowl as necessary. Reduce the speed to low, add the flour and salt, and beat until the mixture comes together as a dough.

4. Form tablespoons of the dough into balls and place them on parchment-lined baking sheets. Place in the oven and bake until firm, about 15 minutes.

5. Sift the remaining cocoa powder into a shallow bowl and use a spatula to transfer a few cookies at a time into the bowl. Roll the cookies around until well coated and then transfer them to wire racks to cool completely.

Yield: 12 Cups

Active Time: 15 Minutes

Total Time: 1 Hour and 15 Minutes

INGREDIENTS

1 cup creamy peanut butter

½ cup confectioners' sugar

½ teaspoon fine sea salt

¼ teaspoon pure vanilla extract

¾ lb. milk chocolate, chopped

Peanut Butter Cups

1. Line a 12-well cupcake pan with paper liners and coat them with nonstick cooking spray. Place the peanut butter, confectioners' sugar, salt, and vanilla in a mixing bowl and stir to combine. Set the mixture aside.

2. Fill a small saucepan with water and bring it to a gentle simmer. Place the chocolate in a heatproof bowl, place it over the simmering water, and stir until it is melted.

3. Place a spoonful of the melted chocolate in each muffin liner and then use a spoon to spread the chocolate halfway up the sides. When you have done this for each liner, place the pan in the refrigerator and let it chill until the chocolate has hardened, 15 to 20 minutes.

4. Remove from the refrigerator, scoop the peanut butter mixture into each chocolate shell, and smooth it with a rubber spatula. Return to the refrigerator and chill for 10 to 15 minutes.

5. Remove from the refrigerator, top each filled shell with another spoonful of melted chocolate, and smooth the top with a rubber spatula. Return to the refrigerator and chill for 25 to 30 minutes before serving.

Peanut Butter Cups

see page 235

Yield: 36 Truffles

Active Time: 20 Minutes

Total Time: 24 Hours

INGREDIENTS

1 lb. dark chocolate (55 to 65 percent)

Pinch of fine sea salt

1¼ cups heavy cream

½ cup cocoa powder

Classic Chocolate Truffles

1. Break the chocolate into small pieces, place it in a food processor, and blitz until it is finely chopped. Place it in a heatproof bowl and add the salt.

2. Place the cream in a saucepan and bring to a simmer over medium heat, stirring frequently. Pour the warm cream over the chocolate and whisk until it has melted and the mixture is smooth. Transfer the chocolate to a square 9-inch baking pan and let it cool completely. Cover with plastic wrap and refrigerate overnight.

3. Line two baking sheets with parchment paper and place the cocoa powder in a shallow bowl. Form heaping tablespoons of the chocolate mixture into balls and roll them in the cocoa powder. Place them on the baking sheets and refrigerate for 30 minutes before serving.

Yield: 24 Servings

Active Time: 15 Minutes

Total Time: 1 Hour and 30 Minutes

INGREDIENTS

¾ cup crushed peppermint candies

¾ lb. semisweet chocolate chips

2 teaspoons canola oil

¾ lb. white chocolate chips

Peppermint Bark

1. Line a rimmed baking sheet with parchment paper and place the crushed peppermint candies in a mixing bowl.

2. Fill a small saucepan halfway with water and bring it to a gentle simmer. Place the semisweet chocolate chips in a heatproof bowl, place it over the simmering water, and stir until melted. Keep the water at a simmer.

3. Stir 1 teaspoon of the canola oil into the melted chocolate and then pour the chocolate onto the baking sheet, using a rubber spatula to distribute evenly. Place in the refrigerator until it has set, about 30 minutes.

4. Place the white chocolate chips in a heatproof bowl, place it over the simmering water, and stir until melted. Stir in the remaining oil and pour the melted white chocolate on top of the hardened semisweet chocolate, using a rubber spatula to distribute evenly.

5. Sprinkle the peppermint pieces liberally over the white chocolate and press down on them lightly. Refrigerate until set, about 30 minutes. Break the bark into pieces and refrigerate until ready to serve.

Yield: 16 Truffles

Active Time: 10 Minutes

Total Time: 2 Hours

INGREDIENTS

½ cup creamy peanut butter

¼ cup honey

¼ teaspoon fine sea salt

4 oz. dark chocolate (55 to 65 percent), chopped

Honey Nut Truffles

1. Place the peanut butter, honey, and salt in a mixing bowl and stir until well combined. Drop teaspoons of the mixture on a parchment-lined baking sheet and then place it in the refrigerator for 1 hour.

2. Remove the baking sheet from the refrigerator. Fill a small saucepan with water and bring it to a gentle simmer. Place the chocolate in a heatproof bowl, place it over the simmering water, and stir until the chocolate has melted.

3. Dip the balls into the melted chocolate until completely covered. Place them back on the baking sheet. When all of the truffles have been coated, place them in the refrigerator and chill until the chocolate is set, about 45 minutes.

Yield: 16 Servings

Active Time: 15 Minutes

Total Time: 2 Hours and 30 Minutes

INGREDIENTS

1 cup chopped walnuts

1 lb. quality bittersweet chocolate, chopped

4 oz. unsalted butter

2 cups sugar

1 teaspoon pure vanilla extract

Chocolate & Walnut Fudge

1. Preheat the oven to 350°F and line a square 8-inch baking pan with heavy-duty aluminum foil, making sure the foil extends over the sides. Coat the foil with nonstick cooking spray.

2. Cover a baking sheet with the walnuts, place it in the oven, and toast the walnuts until they are fragrant and lightly browned, about 5 to 7 minutes. Remove from the oven and set the walnuts aside.

3. Place the chocolate and butter in a heatproof mixing bowl and set aside. Place the sugar in a large saucepan fitted with a candy thermometer and cook over medium heat until it has dissolved and is boiling. Continue to cook, stirring constantly, until the sugar reaches 236°F on a candy thermometer. Carefully pour the sugar over the chocolate-and-butter mixture in the mixing bowl. Whisk until the mixture is smooth and then stir in the toasted walnuts and vanilla.

4. Spread the fudge in an even layer in the baking pan. Refrigerate the fudge until it is set, about 2 hours. Use the foil to lift the fudge out of the pan and cut it into squares.

Yield: 8 to 10 Servings

Active Time: 5 Minutes

Total Time: 50 Minutes

INGREDIENTS

1 cup semisweet chocolate chips

¾ cup creamy peanut butter

1 teaspoon pure vanilla extract

9 cups Rice Chex

1½ cups confectioners' sugar

Muddy Buddies

1. Fill a small saucepan halfway with water and bring it to a gentle simmer. Place the chocolate chips and peanut butter in a heat-proof bowl and microwave on medium for 30 seconds. Remove from the microwave, add the vanilla, and stir until the mixture is smooth.

2. Place the Chex in a large mixing bowl and pour the peanut butter-and-chocolate mixture over the cereal. Carefully stir until all of the Chex are coated.

3. Place the mixture into a large resealable plastic bag and add the confectioners' sugar. Seal the bag and shake until each piece is coated with sugar.

4. Pour the mixture onto a parchment-lined baking sheet. Place the sheet in the refrigerator and chill for 45 minutes before enjoying.

Yield: 4 Servings

Active Time: 25 Minutes

Total Time: 1 Hour

INGREDIENTS

2 cups whole milk

1 (14 oz.) can of unsweetened coconut milk

1 cup heavy cream

Seeds and pod of 1 vanilla bean

2 bananas

¾ cup sugar, plus more to taste

½ fresh coconut

½ cup water

¾ lb. dark chocolate (55 to 65 percent), chopped

Chocolate & Coconut Soup with Brûléed Bananas

1. Place the milk, coconut milk, cream, vanilla seeds, and vanilla pod in a saucepan and bring to a simmer over medium heat. Turn off the heat and let the mixture stand for 20 minutes.

2. Cut the bananas on a bias. Dip one side into a dish of sugar and then use a kitchen torch to caramelize the sugar. Set aside.

3. Preheat the oven to 350°F and line a baking sheet with parchment paper. Remove the outer shell of the coconut and use a spoon to remove the meat. Slice the coconut meat very thin and set aside. In a small saucepan, add the sugar and water and bring to a boil. Remove the syrup from heat and let stand until cool.

4. When the syrup is cool, dip the coconut slices into the syrup and place them on a parchment-lined baking sheet. Place the sheet in the oven and bake until the coconut is golden brown, about 8 minutes. Remove and set aside.

5. After 20 minutes, remove the vanilla pod from the soup and return to a simmer. Turn off the heat, add the chocolate, and stir until the chocolate is melted. Strain the soup through a fine sieve and serve with the bruléed bananas and candied coconut.

APPENDIX

Yield: 2 (9-Inch) Piecrusts

Active Time: 15 Minutes

Total Time: 2 Hours and 15 Minutes

INGREDIENTS

1 cup unsalted butter, cubed

12½ oz. all-purpose flour, plus more as needed

½ teaspoon kosher salt

4 teaspoons sugar

½ cup ice water

Perfect Piecrusts

1. Transfer the butter to a small bowl and place it in the freezer.

2. Place the flour, salt, and sugar in a food processor and pulse a few times until combined.

3. Add the chilled butter and pulse until the mixture is crumbly, consisting of pea-sized clumps.

4. Add the water and pulse until the mixture comes together as a dough.

5. Place the dough on a flour-dusted work surface and fold it over itself until it is a ball. Divide the dough in two and flatten each piece into a 1-inch-thick disc. Envelop each piece in plastic wrap and place in the refrigerator for at least 2 hours before rolling out to fit your pie plate.

Yield: 1 (9-Inch) Crust

Active Time: 10 Minutes

Total Time: 1 Hour

INGREDIENTS

1½ cups graham cracker crumbs

2 tablespoons sugar

1 tablespoon real maple syrup

3 oz. unsalted butter, melted

Graham Cracker Crust

1. Preheat the oven to 375°F. Place the graham cracker crumbs and sugar in a large mixing bowl and stir to combine. Add the maple syrup and 5 tablespoons of the melted butter and stir until thoroughly combined.

2. Grease a 9-inch pie plate with the remaining butter. Pour the dough into the pie plate and gently press into shape. Line the crust with aluminum foil, fill it with uncooked rice, dried beans, or pie weights, and bake for about 10 minutes, until the crust is firm.

3. Remove from the oven, remove the foil and chosen weight, and allow the crust to cool completely before filling.

Yield: 1 (9-inch) Crust

Active Time: 20 Minutes

Total Time: 2 Hours

INGREDIENTS

5 oz. all-purpose flour, plus more as needed

2 tablespoons cocoa powder

2 tablespoons sugar

½ teaspoon fine sea salt

2 oz. unsalted butter

2 tablespoons shortening

1 large egg yolk

2 to 3 tablespoons ice water

Cocoa Crust

1. Place the flour, cocoa powder, sugar, and salt in a food processor and pulse until combined. Add the butter and shortening and pulse until the mixture resembles coarse crumbs. Add the egg yolk and water and pulse until the mixture comes together as a dough.

2. Form the dough into a disc, envelop it in plastic wrap, and refrigerate for 1 hour.

3. Preheat the oven to 350°F. Remove the dough from the refrigerator and let it rest at room temperature for 5 to 10 minutes. Place the dough on a flour-dusted work surface and roll it out to ¼ inch thick. Place the crust in a greased 9-inch pie plate, line it with aluminum foil, and fill it with uncooked rice, dried beans, or pie weights. Place in the oven and bake for 15 to 20 minutes, until firm.

4. Remove from the oven, remove the weight and foil, and let the crust cool completely before filling it.

Yield: 2 (9-Inch) Crusts

Active Time: 15 Minutes

Total Time: 2 Hours and 15 Minutes

INGREDIENTS

1 cup unsalted butter, softened

½ lb. sugar

¼ teaspoon kosher salt

1 egg

2 egg yolks

1 lb. all-purpose flour, plus more as needed

Pâté Sucrée

1. In the work bowl of a stand mixer fitted with the paddle attachment, cream the butter, sugar, and salt on medium speed until the mixture is creamy, light, and fluffy, about 5 minutes.

2. Add the egg and egg yolks and beat until incorporated. Add the flour and beat until the mixture comes together as a dough.

3. Place the dough on a flour-dusted work surface and fold it over itself until it is a ball. Divide the dough in two and flatten each piece into a 1-inch-thick disc. Envelop each piece in plastic wrap and place in the refrigerator for at least 2 hours before rolling it out to fit your pie plate.

Yield: 3 Cups

Active Time: 20 Minutes

Total Time: 30 Minutes

INGREDIENTS

2 cups sugar

½ cup water

8 egg whites

¼ teaspoon fine sea salt

1½ lbs. unsalted butter, softened

1 teaspoon pure vanilla extract

Italian Buttercream

1. Place the sugar and water in a small saucepan, fit it with a candy thermometer, and bring the mixture to a boil.

2. While the syrup is coming to a boil, place the egg whites and salt in the work bowl of a stand mixer fitted with the whisk attachment and whip on medium speed until the mixture holds stiff peaks.

3. Cook the syrup until the thermometer reads 245°F. Immediately remove pan from heat. Once the syrup stops bubbling, let it sit for 30 seconds.

4. Reduce the speed of the mixer to medium-low and slowly pour the syrup down the side of the mixing bowl until all of it has been incorporated. Raise the speed to high and whip until the meringue is glossy and holds stiff peaks.

5. Add the butter 4 oz. at a time and whip until the mixture has thickened.

6. Reduce the speed to medium, add the vanilla, and beat until incorporated.

7. Use immediately, or store in the refrigerator for up to 2 weeks. If refrigerating, return to room temperature before using.

Yield: 3 Cups

Active Time: 10 Minutes

Total Time: 10 Minutes

INGREDIENTS

1 cup unsalted butter, softened

1 cup cream cheese, softened

2 lbs. confectioners' sugar

⅛ teaspoon kosher salt

¼ cup heavy cream

½ teaspoon pure vanilla extract

Cream Cheese Frosting

1. In the work bowl of a stand mixer fitted with the paddle attachment, combine the butter, cream cheese, confectioners' sugar, and salt and beat on low speed until the sugar starts to be incorporated into the butter. Raise the speed to high and beat until the mixture is smooth and fluffy, about 5 minutes.

2. Reduce the speed to low, add the heavy cream and vanilla extract, and beat until incorporated. Use immediately, or store in the refrigerator for up to 2 weeks. If refrigerating, return to room temperature before using.

Yield: 2½ Cups

Active Time: 15 Minutes

Total Time: 2 Hours and 15 Minutes

INGREDIENTS

2 cups whole milk

1 tablespoon unsalted butter

½ cup sugar

3 tablespoons cornstarch

2 large eggs

Pinch of fine sea salt

½ teaspoon pure vanilla extract

Pastry Cream

1. Place the milk and butter in a saucepan and bring to a simmer over medium heat.

2. As the milk mixture is coming to a simmer, place the sugar and cornstarch in a small bowl and whisk to combine. Add the eggs and whisk until the mixture is smooth and creamy.

3. Slowly pour half of the hot milk mixture into the egg mixture and stir until incorporated. Add the salt and vanilla, stir to incorporate, and pour the tempered egg mixture into the saucepan. Cook, while stirring constantly, until the mixture is very thick and about to come to a boil.

4. Remove from heat and pour the pastry cream into a bowl. Place plastic wrap directly on the surface to prevent a skin from forming. Place in the refrigerator and chill for about 2 hours.

Yield: 4 Cups

Active Time: 10 Minutes

Total Time: 10 Minutes

½ lb. marshmallow creme

10 oz. unsalted butter, softened

11 oz. confectioners' sugar

1½ teaspoons pure vanilla extract

¾ teaspoon kosher salt

Butterfluff Filling

1. In the work bowl of a stand mixer fitted with the paddle attachment, cream the marshmallow creme and butter on medium speed until the mixture is light and fluffy, about 5 minutes.

2. Add the confectioners' sugar, vanilla, and salt, reduce the speed to low, and beat for 2 minutes. Use immediately, or store in the refrigerator for up to 1 month.

Yield: 2 Cups

Active Time: 5 Minutes

Total Time: 5 Minutes

INGREDIENTS

2 cups heavy cream

3 tablespoons sugar

1 teaspoon pure vanilla extract

Whipped Cream

1. In the work bowl of a stand mixer fitted with the whisk attachment, whip the heavy cream, sugar, and vanilla on high until the mixture holds soft peaks.

2. Use immediately, or store in the refrigerator for up to 3 days.

INGREDIENTS

½ cup sugar

6 egg yolks

3 tablespoons cornstarch

2 cups whole milk

¼ teaspoon kosher salt

1½ teaspoons pure vanilla
extract

2 oz. unsalted butter,
softened

¼ cup Hazelnut Praline Paste
(see page 257)

Hazelnut Mousseline

1. Place the sugar, egg yolks, and cornstarch in a mixing bowl and whisk for 2 minutes, so that the mixture is thoroughly combined. Set it aside.

2. Place the milk in a medium saucepan and bring it to a simmer over medium heat. While whisking continually, gradually add the warm milk to the egg yolk mixture until it has all been incorporated.

3. Pour the tempered egg yolks into the saucepan and cook over medium heat, stirring constantly. When the custard has thickened and begins to simmer, cook for another 30 seconds and then remove the pan from heat.

4. Whisk in the remaining ingredients, strain the mousseline into a bowl through a fine-mesh sieve, and place plastic wrap directly on the top to keep a skin from forming. Place the mousseline in the refrigerator and chill for 2 hours before using. The mousseline will keep in the refrigerator for 5 days.

Yield: 3 Cups

Active Time: 25 Minutes

Total Time: 2 Hours

2 cups hazelnuts

1 cup sugar

3 tablespoons water

2 teaspoons canola oil

¼ teaspoon fine sea salt

Hazelnut Praline Paste

1. Place the hazelnuts in a large, dry skillet and toast over medium heat until they just start to brown, about 5 minutes. Transfer the nuts to a clean, dry kitchen towel, fold the towel over the nuts, and rub them together until the skins have loosened. Place the toasted nuts on a parchment-lined baking sheet and discard the skins.

2. Place the sugar and water in a small saucepan and warm the mixture over medium heat, swirling the pan occasionally instead of stirring the mixture. Cook until the mixture is a deep golden brown and then pour it over the toasted hazelnuts. Let the mixture sit at room temperature until it has set.

3. Break the hazelnut brittle into pieces, place them in a blender, and add the canola oil and salt. Puree until the mixture is a smooth paste and use immediately or store in the refrigerator.

INGREDIENTS

½ lb. chocolate (dark, milk, or white)

1 cup heavy cream

Chocolate Ganache

1. Place the chocolate in a heatproof mixing bowl and set it aside.

2. Place the heavy cream in a small saucepan and bring to a simmer over medium heat.

3. Pour the cream over the chocolate and let the mixture rest for 1 minute.

4. Gently whisk the mixture until thoroughly combined. Use immediately if drizzling over a cake or serving with fruit. Let the ganache cool for 2 hours if piping. The ganache will keep in the refrigerator for up to 5 days.

Yield: 2 Cups

Active Time: 15 Minutes

Total Time: 15 Minutes

INGREDIENTS

⅔ cup heavy cream

½ cup light corn syrup

⅓ cup dark brown sugar

¼ cup cocoa powder

½ teaspoon fine sea salt

½ lb. bittersweet chocolate, chopped

½ teaspoon espresso powder

2 tablespoons unsalted butter

1 teaspoon pure vanilla extract

Hot Fudge

1. Place the cream, corn syrup, brown sugar, cocoa powder, salt, half of the chocolate, and the espresso powder in a saucepan and cook over medium heat until the chocolate is melted.

2. Reduce the heat and simmer for 5 minutes. Remove the pan from heat and whisk in the remaining chocolate, the butter, and the vanilla. Serve immediately.

Yield: 1½ Cups

Active Time: 20 Minutes

Total Time: 7 Hours

INGREDIENTS

2 cups almonds

1 cup Simple Syrup (see page 260)

1 teaspoon orange blossom water

2 oz. vodka

Orgeat

1. Preheat the oven to 400°F. Place the almonds on a baking sheet, place them in the oven, and toast until they are fragrant, 6 to 8 minutes. Remove the almonds from the oven and let them cool completely.

2. Place the nuts in a food processor and pulse until they are a coarse meal. Set the almonds aside.

3. Place the syrup in a saucepan and warm it over medium heat. Add the almond meal, remove the pan from heat, and let the mixture steep for 6 hours.

4. Strain the mixture through cheesecloth and discard the solids. Stir in the orange blossom water and vodka. Use the orgeat immediately or store it in an airtight container.

Yield: 4 Servings

Active Time: 25 Minutes

Total Time: 24 Hours

INGREDIENTS

24 cherries

Pinch of fine sea salt

¼ cup brandy

Seeds of ½ vanilla bean or 1 teaspoon pure vanilla extract

2 tablespoons demerara sugar

Roasted Vanilla Cherries

1. Place the cherries, salt, brandy, and vanilla in a bowl and let the mixture marinate at room temperature overnight.

2. Preheat the oven to 400°F. Strain the cherries, reserve the liquid, and place the cherries on a baking sheet. Sprinkle the sugar over the cherries, place them in the oven, and roast until the sugar starts to caramelize, 8 to 10 minutes, making sure that the sugar does not burn.

3. Remove the cherries from the oven, pour the reserved liquid over them, and place them back in the oven. Roast for another 5 minutes, remove the cherries from the oven, and let them cool. When they are cool enough to handle, remove the pits from the cherries. Chill the cherries in the refrigerator until ready to use.

Yield: ½ Cup

Active Time: 10 Minutes

Total Time: 1 Hour

INGREDIENTS

½ cup sugar

½ cup water

Simple Syrup

1. Combine the sugar and water in a saucepan and bring the mixture to a boil over medium heat, stirring to dissolve the sugar.

2. When the sugar has dissolved, remove the pan from heat, pour the syrup into a mason jar, and let it cool before using or storing in the refrigerator, where it will keep for up to 1 month.

Yield: 3 Cups

Active Time: 10 Minutes

Total Time: 3 Days

INGREDIENTS

1 piece of burdock root

⅓ oz. cacao nibs

23¾ oz. brandy

Burdock & Cacao Nib Brandy

1. Combine all of the ingredients in a mason jar and let the mixture steep at room temperature for 3 days.

2. Strain and use immediately or store in an airtight container.

Yield: ⅓ Cup

Active Time: 5 Minutes

Total Time: 5 Minutes

INGREDIENTS

2 tablespoons cinnamon

1 tablespoon coriander

1 tablespoon black pepper

1 tablespoon freshly grated nutmeg

1½ teaspoons ground cloves

½ teaspoon ground star anise

Pisto

1. Place all of the ingredients in a bowl and stir to combine. Use immediately or store in an airtight container.

Yield: 2 Cups

Active Time: 15 Minutes

Total Time: 45 Minutes

INGREDIENTS

½ cup evaporated milk

½ cup sugar

1 egg yolk

4 tablespoons unsalted butter, cut into small pieces

Seeds of ½ vanilla bean

½ cup sweetened shredded coconut

½ cup chopped pecans

Coconut & Pecan Frosting

1. Place the evaporated milk, sugar, egg yolk, butter, and vanilla in a medium saucepan and cook over medium heat, stirring frequently, until the mixture has thickened, 10 to 12 minutes.

2. Stir in the coconut and pecans and remove the saucepan from heat. Let the frosting cool completely, stirring occasionally, before using.

Yield: Dough for 16 Croissants

Active Time: 2 Hours

Total Time: 12 Hours

INGREDIENTS

For the Dough

2 tablespoons active dry yeast

1 cup water

1 cup milk

2 oz. sugar

29 oz. all-purpose flour, plus
more as needed

1 tablespoon plus 1 teaspoon
kosher salt

11 oz. unsalted butter,
softened

For the Butter Block

1 lb. unsalted butter, softened

¼ cup all-purpose flour

Croissant Dough

1. To begin preparations for the dough, place the yeast, water, and milk in the work bowl of a stand mixer fitted with the dough hook, gently stir, and let the mixture sit until it starts to foam, about 10 minutes.

2. Add the sugar, flour, and salt and knead the mixture on low until it comes together as a dough, about 5 minutes. Add the butter, continue to knead on low for 2 minutes, and then raise the speed to medium. Knead until the dough is smooth and the butter has been entirely incorporated, 6 to 7 minutes.

3. Spray a mixing bowl with nonstick cooking spray. Transfer the dough to the bowl, cover it with plastic wrap, and chill it in the refrigerator for 3 hours.

4. While the croissant dough is resting, prepare the butter block. Fit the stand mixer with the paddle attachment, add the butter and flour, and beat the mixture until smooth.

5. Transfer the mixture to a Silpat mat that is in a baking sheet. Use a small spatula to spread the mixture into a 7 x 10–inch rectangle.

6. Place the baking sheet in the refrigerator for 30 minutes to 1 hour. You want the butter block to be firm but pliable. If the butter block is too firm for the following steps, let the butter sit at room temperature for a few minutes.

7. Remove the dough from the refrigerator, place it on a flour-dusted work surface, and roll it into a 10 x 20–inch rectangle.

8. Place the butter block in the center of the dough. Fold the dough over the butter block like a letter, folding a third of the dough from the left side of the dough and a third from the right so that they meet in the center. Pinch the seam to seal.

9. Turn the dough 90 degrees clockwise and flip it over so that the seam is facing down. Roll out the dough into a 10 x 20–inch rectangle. Make another letter fold of the dough, place the dough on the Silpat mat, and cover it with plastic wrap. Chill in the refrigerator for 1 hour.

10. Place the dough on a flour-dusted work surface, roll it into a 10 x 20–inch rectangle, and fold the dough like a letter, lengthwise. Pinch the seam to seal, turn the dough 90 degrees clockwise, and flip the dough over so that the seam is facing down. Place the dough back on the baking sheet, cover it in plastic wrap, and refrigerate for 1 hour.

11. Place the dough on a flour-dusted work surface, roll it into a 10 x 20–inch rectangle, and fold the dough like a letter, lengthwise. Pinch the seam to seal, turn the dough 90 degrees clockwise, and flip the dough over so that the seam is facing down. Place the dough back on the baking sheet, cover it in plastic wrap, and refrigerate for 4 hours. After this period of rest, the dough will be ready to make croissants with.

METRIC CONVERSIONS

US Measurement	Approximate Metric Liquid Measurement	Approximate Metric Dry Measurement
1 teaspoon	5 ml	5 g
1 tablespoon or ½ ounce	15 ml	14 g
1 ounce or ⅛ cup	30 ml	29 g
¼ cup or 2 ounces	60 ml	57 g
⅓ cup	80 ml	76 g
½ cup or 4 ounces	120 ml	113 g
⅔ cup	160 ml	151 g
¾ cup or 6 ounces	180 ml	170 g
1 cup or 8 ounces or ½ pint	240 ml	227 g
1½ cups or 12 ounces	350 ml	340 g
2 cups or 1 pint or 16 ounces	475 ml	454 g
3 cups or 1½ pints	700 ml	680 g
4 cups or 2 pints or 1 quart	950 ml	908 g

About Cider Mill Press Book Publishers

Good ideas ripen with time. From seed to harvest, Cider Mill Press brings fine reading, information, and entertainment together between the covers of its creatively crafted books. Our Cider Mill bears fruit twice a year, publishing a new crop of titles each spring and fall.

"Where Good Books Are Ready for Press"
501 Nelson Place
Nashville, Tennessee 37214

cidermillpress.com